VIBRANT CHURCH

BECOMING A HEALTHY CHURCH IN THE 21ST CENTURY

THOM S. RAINER
& DANIEL L. AKIN

LEARNING ACTIVITIES AND LEADER GUIDE BY ART CRISCOE

LifeWay Press®
NASHVILLE, TENNESSEE

Published by LifeWay Press®
© 2008 Thom S. Rainer and Daniel L. Akin

No part of this book may be reproduced or transmitted in any form or by any means, electronic or mechanical, including photocopying and recording, or by any information storage or retrieval system, except as may be expressly permitted in writing by the publisher. Requests for permission should be addressed in writing to LifeWay Press®; One LifeWay Plaza; Nashville, TN 37234-0175.

ISBN 978-1-4158-6541-5
Item 005125346

This book is the resource for course CG-1376 in the subject areas The Church and Ministry in the Christian Growth Study Plan.

Dewey decimal classification: 262
Subject headings: CHURCH \ BAPTISTS—DOCTRINES

Unless otherwise noted, Scripture quotations are taken from the Holman Christian Standard Bible®, copyright © 1999, 2000, 2002, 2003 by Holman Bible Publishers. Used by permission. Scripture quotations marked NIV are taken from the Holy Bible, New International Version, copyright © 1973, 1978, 1984 by International Bible Society. Scripture quotations marked NASB are taken from the New American Standard Bible®, Copyright © 1960, 1962, 1963, 1968, 1971, 1972, 1973, 1975, 1977, 1995 by The Lockman Foundation. Used by permission. *(www.lockman.org)* The quotation from *The Message* is taken from Eugene H. Peterson, *The Message* (Colorado Springs: NavPress, 1995).

We believe that the Bible has God for its author; salvation for its end; and truth, without any mixture of error, for its matter and that all Scripture is totally true and trustworthy. The 2000 statement of *The Baptist Faith and Message* is our doctrinal guideline.

To order additional copies of this resource, write to LifeWay Church Resources Customer Service; One LifeWay Plaza; Nashville, TN 37234-0113; phone toll free (800) 458-2772; fax order to (615) 251-5933; e-mail *orderentry@lifeway.com;* order online at *www.lifeway.com;* or visit the LifeWay Christian Store serving you.

Printed in the United States of America

Leadership and Adult Publishing
LifeWay Church Resources
One LifeWay Plaza
Nashville, TN 37234-0175

CONTENTS

THE AUTHORS

 Thom S. Rainer is the president and chief executive officer of LifeWay Christian Resources in Nashville, Tennessee. Prior to assuming this position in 2006, Rainer was the dean of the Billy Graham School of Missions, Evangelism, and Church Growth at the Southern Baptist Theological Seminary, where he had previously served as a professor of evangelism and church growth.

As the president and chief executive officer of the Rainer Group, Inc., from 1988 to 2005, Rainer consulted with more than five hundred churches, documenting and reporting on ministry trends in evangelical churches. His books include *Simple Church* (coauthor), *Breakout Churches*, *The Unchurched Next Door*, *Surprising Insights from the Unchurched*, *High-Expectation Churches*, *The Every-Church Guide to Growth* (coauthor), *Encyclopedia of Evangelism and Church Growth* (coeditor), and *Effective Evangelistic Churches*. He has provided consultation to numerous periodicals and news services, including *USA Today*, *Time*, Associated Press, and Religious News Service. Rainer has also served as the senior pastor of churches in Alabama, Florida, Kentucky, and Indiana.

A native of Alabama, Rainer holds a B.S. from the University of Alabama and an M.Div. and Ph.D. from the Southern Baptist Theological Seminary. He and his wife have three grown sons.

 Daniel L. Akin is the president of Southeastern Baptist Theological Seminary in Wake Forest, North Carolina. Formerly, he was the vice-president for academic administration, the dean of the school of theology, and a professor of theology and preaching at the Southern Baptist Theological Seminary in Louisville, Kentucky. Prior to joining the staff of Southern Seminary, Akin taught New Testament, theology, and church history at the Criswell College and was a professor of theology and the dean of students at Southeastern Seminary.

Akin is the author of *God on Sex*, *Discovering the Biblical Jesus*, *John's Letters*, and *1, 2, 3 John* in *New American Commentary*. He has contributed to the books *The Baptist Faith and Message 2000*, *The Mission of Today's Church*, *Harmony of the Gospels*, *Perspectives on Church Government*, *Pastoral Leadership for Manhood and Womanhood*, *Holman Old Testament Commentary*, and others. He has also served as the editor of *The Believer's Study Bible*, *The Southern Baptist Journal of Theology*, and *A Theology for the Church*.

Akin holds a B.A. in biblical studies from the Criswell College, an M.Div. from Southwestern Baptist Theological Seminary, and a Ph.D. in humanities from the University of Texas at Arlington. He and his wife have four grown sons.

The learning activities and leader guides were written by Art Criscoe. Retired from LifeWay Christian Resources, Criscoe is a curriculum developer and writer for Christ to the World Ministries, an international missions organization. Criscoe has served as the pastor of churches in Texas, South Carolina, and Tennessee and as an academic dean and a professor of Bible and Christian education at Columbia Bible College in South Carolina.

INTRODUCTION

"Now to Him who is able to do above and beyond all that we ask or think—according to the power that works in you—to Him be glory in the church and in Christ Jesus to all generations, forever and ever. Amen."

Ephesians 3:20-21

MEET MARK AND JIM

When Mark Ryder asked his coworker, Jim Tracy, to visit his church, he never expected to get a positive response. But much to Mark's surprise, Jim enthusiastically accepted. "I've been thinking about visiting a church anyway," Jim commented. "I guess I would feel more comfortable attending with you."

The two men decided to have lunch together after the church service the next Sunday. When the entrée was served, Mark eagerly asked his friend about his experience. "You know," Jim said as he began to cut his grilled chicken, "I liked your church. It reminded me how much I have missed in the past few years."

Jim then shared with Mark that he became a Christian as a teenager but dropped out of church when he went to college. "I'm getting married in four months," Jim said. "My fiancée is a committed Christian, and she wants us to start our marriage right by getting connected with a church. I will probably do that, but I still have questions about the church—any church. Do I really need to belong to a church to be a good Christian? Why can't I practice my faith without attending church? What does the church really do anyway? What is the purpose of the church? Does the church really matter today?"

Jim looked at Mark's wide eyes and knew that his rapid-fire questions had caught his friend off guard. But Jim's questions about the church were good. Look at them again.

In this book we will follow Mark and Jim's attempt to understand what a church is. In doing so, we will try to answer tough questions about the church and identify factors that make a church healthy. We have used the title *Vibrant Church* to capture the essence of a healthy church.

We hope by the time you finish this book, you will have a better grasp of this commonly misunderstood entity called the church.

STARTING POINTS

Vibrant Church is a study of one of the most important doctrines of the Bible and one of the most crucial topics in Christianity today: the doctrine of ecclesiology, or the study of church. The nature of a biblical, New Testament church is a discussion that devoted followers of the Lord Jesus cannot ignore. After all, Christ said in Matthew 16:18, "I will build My church and the forces of Hades will not overpower it," and Paul reminded us in Acts 20:28 that the body of believers is "the church of God, which He purchased with His own blood." Obviously, the church is important to the Lord. Therefore, it must be important to us as well.

The doctrine of the church is a hot topic in our own day, especially the question of what characterizes a healthy or vibrant church. Put this question on the table, and you may get as many answers as there are participants in the debate! In this book our goal is to be rigorously biblical while at the same time being relevant and practical. We will attempt to present sound theology in a way that is easy to understand, and then we will provide some insights and suggestions for how we can be the church of the Lord Jesus Christ in a 21st-century context.

In the previous paragraph find the synonym for *vibrant*.
Write that word in the following sentence.

A vibrant church is a _____ church.

This doctrinal study will help you understand what the Bible teaches about a healthy church.

On one hand, it is interesting to note that in a real sense, the 21st century is much like the 1st century in terms of religious pluralism and spirituality. This is just one reason a faithful theology of the church must be grounded in Scripture.

On the other hand, the 21st century is utterly unique. We are a global village that is driven by international posturing, political turmoil, and technological advances. We can hardly keep up with all the changes that are taking place. However, we *must* keep up if we are to engage our world effectively with the life-changing gospel of Jesus Christ. We will have to stand on certain nonnegotiable, bedrock principles if we are to be true to Christ. At the same time, we must be in touch with diverse cultures and sensitive to our particular context if we are to share the good news of the gospel in a way that modern people can understand and embrace.

ANSWERING JIM'S QUESTIONS

Jim had some very good questions. We will attempt to answer his questions and others in this book.

> Turn back to page 6 and underline the five questions
> Jim asked. Think about how you would answer them.

Our study will be divided into six chapters that address six questions related to the doctrine of the church. We pray that the answers we provide will promote a healthy, vibrant church life. These six chapters are as follows.

1. *Just What Is the Church Anyway?* In this opening chapter we will look at the basic nature and essence of the church. In doing so, we will examine some New Testament images that will help us understand what the church is supposed to be.

2. *Is My Church Is Acting like the Church?* Combining biblical theology and historical church practice, we will examine the essential marks of a New Testament church, such as a regenerate membership and observance of the ordinances.

3. *How Does a Vibrant Church Make Decisions?* This chapter will be a must-read for those who are interested in the elder-versus-nonelder debate. But we will focus primarily on organizational issues for church health that are biblically grounded.

4. *Does My Church Have to Practice Church Discipline?* This is an often-avoided topic but one the church can no longer afford to neglect. Just what does the Bible say about this issue?

5. *How Does a Vibrant Church Carry Out Its Main Purposes?* Here we will survey Scripture for essential patterns and practices. Special attention will be given to the way we preach and teach the Bible. We will also consider the concept that a church must have clear purposes. Are they biblical or just pragmatic?

6. *What Should a Vibrant Church Look like in the 21st Century?* In the final chapter we will focus on essential characteristics of a New Testament church. Finally, as Mark and Jim draw some conclusions for

the church today, we will help you apply what you have learned to your own church.

Jim's questions motivated Mark to begin a serious study of the church for himself. And much to Mark's surprise, Jim asked to join him in this study. We will listen to the fascinating conversations between these two men. They will ask many questions about the role of the church today. These are serious questions for serious times.

Here are four suggested goals for your study of this book.

1. You will understand the nature of the church and its distinctive characteristics, along with how it is organized and how it carries out its mission.
2. You will be able to identify the blessings and benefits of church membership.
3. You will gain a deeper appreciation and love for the church.
4. You will strengthen your commitment to the church.

Each chapter suggests a Scripture passage for you to memorize that supports the topic of study. Take time to do this. Read the passage over and over and say it aloud until you can quote it from memory. Write the Scripture on a card and carry it with you to review throughout the week. When you hide God's Word in your heart, it can never be taken from you. Memorizing Scripture follows the practice of God's people in the Old Testament and the early Christians in the New Testament.

Study with an open Bible. Take time to read the Scripture passages referred to. Pattern your study after the Beroeans of long ago, who "welcomed the message with eagerness and examined the Scriptures daily to see if these things were so" (Acts 17:11).

Make prayer an integral part of your study. Jesus said, "When the Spirit of truth comes, He will guide you into all the truth" (John 16:13). The Holy Spirit, who lives within you, will open your heart to God's truth. Ask God to help you apply to your daily life what you learn.

We pray that God will be glorified in this study and that He will use it to strengthen, energize, and equip God's people to be the church in the 21st century. We pray that your church can be a vibrant church, not just another institution going through the motions. The need is great, but our God is greater! Let's be the church and storm the gates of Hades together for the honor of our Head, the Lord Jesus Christ.

Chapter 1

JUST WHAT IS THE CHURCH ANYWAY?

Learning Goal

After studying this chapter, you will understand the meaning, essence, and nature of the church.

Memory Verse

"You are a chosen race, a royal priesthood, a holy nation, a people for His possession, so that you may proclaim the praises of the One who called you out of darkness into His marvelous light" (1 Pet. 2:9).

What began as a series of questions over lunch became a serious quest for Mark and Jim. They were determined to find out whether people attend church from habit and tradition or from genuine commitment. They agreed to begin studying to answer the basic question "Just what is the church anyway?"

"I have to admit that I'm a skeptic," Jim shared with Mark. "I've been out of church for so many years that I really wonder whether I'm missing anything."

Mark listened to his unchurched friend and responded carefully: "Jim, I think your doubts about the local church are based on your observations of weak or unbiblical churches. In our first study let's see what the Bible says about the church. Then we can compare our information to what we see in churches today."

"OK. Maybe it would help me to know what church means to you," Jim responded.

"You can probably remember from when we were kids in church that the common definition for *church* was *a group of baptized believers*," Mark began. "That was one way of saying that the church is not the building but the people who meet there. But even that definition is more complex than it appears on the surface. It seems to suggest that all believers are baptized—something we'll talk about later. And it seems to imply that all baptized believers are active in a local church. That hasn't applied to you in recent years, and it doesn't apply to a lot of people these days—another topic we'll deal with later. But it does show us that simple definitions from our past don't explain everything today. Let's see what we can learn about what God intended the church to be."

And so the first week of the search for the vibrant church began.

Briefly describe two of your earliest memories of church.

1. *I can REMEMBER THE PREACHER Calling People to the Alter For SALVATION.*

2. *FisH Frys & cookouts. PrAise teams AND Ministry obligation Services.*

BASIC MEANINGS OF *CHURCH*

In attempting to define *church*, you can expect a variety of different answers.

How would you define *church*? *God institution to Reach the lost that has been separated From him due to our sin.*

Some people think of church only as a building—the place they pass on their way to work. Some people think of it as an activity—what their neighbors do on Sunday. Others think of church as a denomination: "My grandmother is a member of the Methodist Church." Some people think of it as a religion that is theirs by birth. Just as they were born in Northern Ireland and are therefore Irish, they are Catholic by birth as well.

Multiple usages of the term *church* abound, and yet there is a lack of clarity at a more basic level—a lack of understanding about the essence and nature of the church. Millard Erickson helps us understand the problem we face: "[God] is no longer viewed as relating to the world only through the agency of his supernatural institution, the church, but also dynamically relating to the world through many avenues or institutions. [The emphasis is on what God is doing, not on what he is like.] Consequently, more attention is given to the mission of the church than to its identity."[1] This is especially true in America.

Some people think of church only as a building.

Erickson is correct. We first need to understand what it means to be the church and then focus on what it means to do church. We believe the issue is urgent if the church is going to fulfill the mission to which God has called it. Let's start by getting a handle on the terminology. Then we'll look at the New Testament church and finally at what the church is and is not as we define it today.

THE ENGLISH TERM *CHURCH*

The word *church*, along with the Scottish word *kirk* and the German *kirche*, is derived from the Greek *kuriakon*, which means *belonging to the Lord*. *Kuriakon* occurs only twice in the New Testament, neither time with reference to the church as commonly used today. In 1 Corinthians 11:20 the word refers to the Lord's Supper and in Revelation 1:10 to the Lord's Day. Its application to the church stems from its use by early Christians for the place where they met together, denoting it as a place belonging to God. The term was applied to the assembly itself. The church was not a building but a meeting or gathering of God's people in an open, visible assembly.

Every time I see or hear the word *church*, I think of the descriptive phrase *belonging to the Lord*. This wonderful phrase reminds us that God loves us and provides for us. We are His, and He is ours.

Kuriakon *(Greek):* **belonging to the Lord**

Spend a few minutes thinking not just about your church as belonging to the Lord but also about your life as belonging to the Lord. Answer the following questions.

Does my life truly belong to the Lord?

☑ Yes ○ No STRIVING FOR THIS DAILY

Do other people know that I belong to the Lord?

☑ Yes ○ No

Does belonging to the Lord make a difference in my life?

☑ Yes ○ No

Does my marriage belong to the Lord? NOT MARRIED. MY SINGLENESS DOES

○ Yes ○ No

Does my family belong to the Lord?

☑ Yes ○ No

Does my health belong to the Lord?

☑ Yes ○ No

Do my possessions belong to the Lord?
☑ Yes ○ No

Does my money belong to the Lord?
☑ Yes ○ No *HARD AREA.*

Does my work, my career, belong to the Lord?
☑ Yes ○ No

Does my time belong to the Lord?
☑ Yes ○ No *I FEEL LIKE THERE IS NOT ENOUGH TIME*

Do my hobbies belong to the Lord?
☑ Yes ○ No

Select one area of your life from the questions above. Describe one thing you can do to devote that area more fully to the Lord.

THIS AREA WOULD BE MY TIME IN THE MORNINGS WHEN I GET UP. God NEEDS TO BE FIRST ON MY MIND TO GIVE THANKS & PRAISE TOO.

BIBLICAL TERMS FOR *CHURCH*

The church is clearly a New Testament concept, but a look at the ways God related to His people in the Old Testament can give depth to our understanding of the New Testament church.

> God's eternal plan has always been to display His glory through a particular group of people.

God's eternal plan has always been to display His glory through a particular group of people. In Exodus 19 we are told that God chose Israel to be His people, to carry His name: "In the third month, on the same day of the month that the Israelites had left the land of Egypt, they entered the Wilderness of Sinai. … Moses went up the mountain to God, and the Lord called to him from the mountain: 'This is what you must say to the house of Jacob, and explain to the Israelites: You have seen what I did to the Egyptians and how I carried you on eagles' wings and brought you to Me. Now if you will listen to Me and carefully keep My covenant, you will be My own possession out of all the peoples, although all the earth is Mine, and you will be My kingdom of priests and My holy nation' " (vv. 1,3-6).

Identify three terms God in the previous passage that God used to describe the Israelites.

1. _____

2. _____

3. _____

The Old Testament identifies the people of God with specific terms. The Hebrew word *qahal* is defined as *an assembly, a congregation, or a convocation* (see Gen. 35:11, 49:6; Num. 22:4; Ezra 10:12; Ps. 89:6; Prov. 5:14; Jer. 31:8; Mic. 2:5). A second word, *edâh*, means *a congregation, a company assembled together by appointment, or acting concertedly.* John Hammett points out the distinction between the two terms: "*Qahal* embraces only those who have heard the call and are following it. *Edâh*, on the other hand, is the permanent community into which one was born."[2] Although these terms predate the church, they point to the existence of a people whom God called together for His purposes.

The church was born on the day of Pentecost (see Acts 2). In the New Testament the Greek word for church is *ekklesia*. It is derived from the verb *ekkaleo*, a compound of *ek*, meaning *out*, and *kaleo, to call*. Often the meaning is used to support the biblical doctrine of the church as a people called out by God and separated from the world. Though this is theologically true, the usage of the term in the secular Greek language does not support this meaning. *Ekklesia* "came to stand for any assembly, regardless of its constituents or manner of convening. This broad use is evident even in the New Testament where a confused mob which had rushed into the theater at Ephesus is twice called an *ekklesia* (Acts 19:32,41), and in the same context the term is used for 'a lawful assembly' (v. 39)."[3] In secular Greek *ekklesia* referred only to the assembly or meeting and never to the people who composed that assembly. When the people were not assembled, they were not considered an *ekklesia*. A new *ekklesia* came to be each time the people assembled. So while today we think of *ekklesia* as referring specifically to the New Testament church, at that time the word had more than one meaning. Just as person-on-the-street interviews today asking people to define the word *church* would not

Qahal *(Hebrew):*
an assembly, a congregation, or a convocation

Edâh *(Hebrew):*
congregation, a company assembled together by appointment, or acting concertedly

Ekklesia *(Greek):*
called out

yield uniform answers, the same confusion may well have existed when a New Testament believer used the word *ekklesia*.

The church was born (check the correct response)—
○ with the people Israel in the Old Testament;
○ during the ministry of John the Baptist;
○ on the day of Pentecost;
○ during the ministry of Paul.

"There are 114 occurrences of *ekklesia* in the New Testament. Five of these have no reference to the New Testament church, leaving 109 that are so related. …The word does not occur in the Gospels except for three references in Matthew 16:18; 18:17. It is also absent from 2 Timothy, Titus, 1 Peter, 2 Peter, 1 John, 2 John, and Jude."[4]

As we read the New Testament, we discover "a development of the term *ekklesia* from the simple non-technical meaning of assembly to the full technical designation for the Christian people of God."[5] A survey of the New Testament reveals four clear uses of the term *ekklesia* to refer to a church or churches.

As you continue reading, underline the description of church in each of the following uses.

The local church. Most often, the word *ekklesia* designates a specific gathering of believers in a definite locality. This is the term's primary usage in the New Testament.

A house church. In some cases the word denotes what may be called a domestic *ekklesia*, the church in the house of an individual (see Philem. 2). The early church often met in homes.

A collection of churches. Here the term refers to the churches of a region, for example, Judea, Galilee, and Samaria (see Acts 9:31). This use is very rare.

The universal church. In some instances the word denotes the whole body of Christ, all believers throughout the world, those who outwardly profess Christ and organize for purposes of worship under the guidance of appointed officers. This emphasis is found in the Books of Ephesians and Colossians. In Ephesians 1:22-23 the church is referred to as Christ's body. The character of this group is 100 percent regenerate. It includes every

---

"To Philemon, our dear friend and co-worker, to Apphia our sister, to Archippus our fellow soldier, and to the church that meets in your house."

Philemon 1-2

"The church throughout all Judea, Galilee, and Samaria had peace, being built up and walking in the fear of the Lord and in the encouragement of the Holy Spirit, and it increased in numbers."

Acts 9:31

believer in every place on earth as well as those who are in heaven (see Heb. 12:23). Here the church constitutes the redeemed of all the ages.

The universal church is sometimes referred to as the invisible church. However, the New Testament never speaks of an invisible church. Members of a local church are real, visible people; and so are members of the universal church. Saucy notes, "Even this invisible membership is very visible in the reality of life. As for membership in an invisible church without fellowship with any local assembly, this concept is never contemplated in the New Testament. The universal church was the universal fellowship of believers who met visibly in local assemblies."[6] The one universal church may be manifested in a particular place; "yet each individual assembly is the church in that place."[7]

Uses of *ekklesia* in the New Testament:
- **Local church**
- **House church**
- **Collection of churches**
- **Universal church**

Define each term in your own words.

Local church: _____

_____

_____

House church: _____

_____

_____

Collection of churches: _____

_____

_____

Universal church: _____

_____

_____

Read each Scripture reference and match it with the correct term for *church*.

___ 1. 1 Corinthians 1:1-3   a. Local church

___ 2. Ephesians 5:27

___ 3. Colossians 4:15   b. House church

___ 4. Acts 9:31

___ 5. 1 Corinthians 16:19b   c. Collection of churches

___ 6. Acts 13:1-3

___ 7. Acts 11:25-26   d. Universal church

Answers: 1. a, 2. d, 3. b,

4. c, 5. b, 6. a, 7. a

CORRECTIVES IN DEFINING *CHURCH*

Robert Saucy notes that the word *church* "has extended to various contemporary uses: (1) a place of meeting, (2) a local organization of believers, (3) the universal body of believers, (4) a particular denomination, for example, the Lutheran Church, and (5) an organization of believers related to a particular area or nation, for example, the Church of England."[8] Unfortunately, not all of these uses have a biblical basis.

The church is not a building. Nowhere in the New Testament does the word *ekklesia* refer to a building. The *ekklesia* of the New Testament is never a structure composed of stones and lime or bricks and mortar. A statement such as "I pass by the church every day on my way to work" would have made no sense to the writers of the New Testament. The church is the body of believers in Jesus wherever they meet for worship, witness, and work. In the early days gatherings were small; and believers, as previously mentioned, often met in homes (see Rom. 16:5; Col. 4:15; Philem. 2).

> The church is the body of believers in Jesus wherever they meet for worship, witness, and work.

The church is not a state church. When a nation has a state church, all citizens are by birth members of the church as long as they do not explicitly leave it. Constantine formed the first state church in A.D. 313 by making Christianity the official religion of the Roman Empire. During the Reformation Martin Luther rebelled against the official state church, the Catholic Church. Nevertheless, the church he established, the Lutheran Church, later became the state church of Germany. Some countries still have state religions today, such as Norway, which has Lutheranism as its state church, and England, which has the Anglican Church.

The concept of a state church is completely foreign to the New Testament. Such an institution severely compromises voluntary, responsible commitment by individuals to a local body of believers; and the result is an unregenerate membership—baptized heathens.

The church is not a denomination. The New Testament describes no organization on a broader level than the local church. Scripture does not explicitly command local churches of an area to form a union, nor does it furnish us with an example of such a union. However, Acts 15 records evidence of Paul's relief collection for the church in Jerusalem (see 2 Cor. 8–9). This example supports voluntary cooperation, mutual interaction, and encouragement for more effective ministry and missions among groups of local churches.

This biblical principle undergirds our efforts as Southern Baptists. We cooperate for more effective ministry to meet human needs. Baptist churches are autonomous, or independent; they can choose to join with other churches on the associational, state, or national level for ministry and missions efforts; but each local church is free to make this choice. These voluntary organizations of churches may contribute funds to do together what one church cannot do on its own, but no regional or national organization dictates the governance or financial control of a local church. However, an organization of churches can make the decision to admit a church or to refuse to allow a church to affiliate with the organization if the church is deemed to be out of step with biblical theology or practice.

Check each statement that reflects the primary meaning of *church* in the New Testament.
○ 1. She belongs to the Methodist Church.
○ 2. Our church increased its missions giving.
○ 3. Lutheranism is the state church in Norway.
○ 4. The church is located at Broadway and Vine.
○ 5. The church voted to build a new educational building.
○ 6. Our church has a strong evangelistic ministry.
○ 7. The church in South Korea is strong.

We checked 2, 5, and 6. In each of these statements, the reference is to the local body of believers. With respect to number 4, when the body of believers meets at Broadway and Vine, the church is there. The rest of the time, only the building is there.

BIBLICAL IMAGES OF THE CHURCH

Biblical images can teach us much about the essence and nature of the church. John Hammett believes it can be argued that "this is the primary means by which we are instructed."[9] We will highlight three prominent New Testament images of the church.

Biblical images of the church:

• **People of God**

• **Body of Christ**

• **Temple of the Holy Spirit**

"You are a chosen race, a royal priesthood, a holy nation, a people for His possession, so that you may proclaim the praises of the One who called you out of darkness into His marvelous light."

1 Peter 2:9

THE PEOPLE OF GOD

Is there continuity between the nation of Israel and the church? In 1 Peter 2:9 the church is called "a chosen race, a royal priesthood, a holy nation, a people for His possession." This language recalls descriptions of Israel in Exodus 19:5-6; Deuteronomy 4:20; 7:6; Hosea 1:10; 2:23; and other places throughout the Old Testament where God calls Israel "My people."

In Exodus 19 God first called the nation of Israel to be His chosen people: "If you will listen to Me and carefully keep My covenant, you will be My own possession out of all the peoples, although all the earth is Mine, and you will be My kingdom of priests and My holy nation" (vv. 5-6). Continuity is further suggested in the biblical promise "I will be their God, and they will be My people" (Jer. 31:33). However, only after Pentecost (see Acts 2) were God's people called the church. The indwelling Holy Spirit (see John 14:15-17) made this people different in some sense from the Old Testament people of God. Jesus' death and resurrection and the Spirit's coming at Pentecost inaugurated a new day for the people of God.

Hammett summarizes insight provided by the image "people of God":

1. It gives the church a connection to the redeemed in the Old Testament and God's great purpose of calling a people to Himself.

2. It underscores the nature of the church as called; it is called by God to be His people. God took the initiative in calling a people to Himself.

3. The church is a people, not a collection of isolated individuals.

4. The church is God's people, not a human institution.
   • As God's people, the church is called to be holy and loving.
   • As God the Father's people, the church is a family.

- As God the Son's people, the church is composed of those who believe in Christ.
- As God the Spirit's people, the church is those who experience His indwelling and fellowship.[10]

"The people of God" is a powerful image of who the church is. We are people who belong to the Lord God Himself.

List the four terms for *church* in 1 Peter 2:9 (margin, p. 20).

1. _____

2. _____

3. _____

4. _____

> *"We were all baptized by one Spirit into one body—whether Jews or Greeks, whether slaves or free— and we were all made to drink of one Spirit."*
>
> 1 Corinthians 12:13

THE BODY OF CHRIST

This image appears in four of Paul's letters—Romans, 1 Corinthians, Ephesians, and Colossians. In Romans and 1 Corinthians the body of Christ is an image for the local church. The emphasis is on the relationships that members of the body have with one another (see 1 Cor. 12:27). The local church is regarded as the body of Christ in a particular place.

Unity in the body. The body image in Romans and 1 Corinthians highlights unity, the common experience of baptism by or in the one Spirit (see 1 Cor. 12:13). It also emphasizes unity in diversity (see Rom. 12:4-5; 1 Cor. 12:14-20). Paul reminded the Romans that it is only "in Christ" that we are "individually members of one another" (Rom. 12:5). The supernatural power of a shared life in Christ and a common reception of the Spirit are required to overcome the divisions of Greek and Jew, slave and free, male and female. There can be diversity of race and sex and social status, diversity in function and gift; but there is one body, one Spirit, one Lord, one faith (see Eph. 4:4-5).

Mutuality in the body. The body metaphor also teaches mutuality of love and care for all within the body. Romans 12:5 says that in Christ we are "individually members of one another." First Corinthians 12 shows

> *"As we have many parts in one body, and all the parts do not have the same function, in the same way we who are many are one body in Christ and individually members of one another."*
>
> Romans 12:4-5

that each part of the body needs every other part, pointing out that God desires all members of the body to "have the same concern for each other" (v. 25). Mutuality is also reflected in more than 30 "one another" passages in the New Testament, such as "love one another" and "forgive one another."

Complementing these insights, Hammett notes that

> in Ephesians and Colossians, the image of the body of Christ is used, but in a totally different context, with different emphases. ... [Here] the body is related to the universal church. Five times Paul places the two together: "the church ... his body" (Ephesians 1:22-23; 5:23,29-30; Col. 1:18,24). In each case, the description of the church points to and virtually requires the universal sense. However, while the universal church does seem to fit the usage of *ekklesia* in these two letters, the activities Paul describes (of pastors and teachers equipping God's people, of the body growing as each part does its work; see Eph. 4:12,16; Col. 2:19) take place in local churches and thus local assemblies are not totally out of view.[11]

He is also the head of the body. Hammett also points out that "in Ephesians and Colossians, a new element is added to the usage of the body image, that of the relationship of the head to the body. In these letters, a major emphasis is on the role and importance of Christ, who is identified as the head of the body five times (see Eph. 1:22; 4:15; 5:23; Col. 1:18; 2:19). ... The teaching on Christ as the head of the body highlights the ideas of his *authority* over the body and his *provision* for the body. His provision for the body leads to its *growth*."[12]

"He is also the head of the body, the church; He is the beginning, the first-born from the dead, so that He might come to have first place in everything."

Colossians 1:18

As the head of His church, Christ is supreme or preeminent in everything (see Col. 1:18). However, His authority is described as loving and sacrificial in the beautiful comparison of Christ and the church to a husband and a wife (see Eph. 5:22-33). Christ, as the head, exercises His authority on behalf of the church, loving her, giving Himself up for her, feeding her, and caring for her.

Hammett's summary of this metaphor is again helpful:

1. The image of the body points to the church's unity, seen especially in the ordinances of the Lord's Supper and believer's baptism. [The ordinances will be discussed in a later chapter.]
2. The image of the body aptly illustrates how the church may be one, while its members are diverse. We are a unity with diversity.
3. The body image reflects how the members of the church should show mutual love and care for one another.
4. Christ, as the head of the body, is the ultimate authority for the church. His will is to be sought in all things.
5. As head, Christ also provides for the needs of the church. We are completely dependent on Him.
6. Christlikeness is the goal of the church's growth; all members of the church contribute to the growth and unity of the church as all perform their own particular ministries (Eph. 4:11-16).[13]

Christ, as the head of the body, is the ultimate authority for the church.

Describe ways your church reflects the image of the body of Christ in the following areas.

Worship: _____

_____

_____

Fellowship: _____

_____

_____

Ministry: _____

_____

_____

"Don't you know that you are God's sanctuary and that the Spirit of God lives in you?"

1 Corinthians 3:16

Naos *(Greek):* the innermost sanctuary, the place of God's dwelling

Priesthood of believers: the belief that every Christian has direct access to God through Christ without a human mediator and that every Christian is to serve as a priest on behalf of others

Answers: 1. c, 2. a, 3. b

THE TEMPLE OF THE HOLY SPIRIT

In 1 Corinthians 3:9 Paul compares the church to a field and a building. He goes on to state that the foundation of the building is Jesus Christ (v. 11). But in verse 16 he sees the church as a very special building, God's temple. Elsewhere Paul speaks of the individual Christian's body as the temple of the Holy Spirit (see 1 Cor. 6:19). The church is the temple of God by means of the indwelling Holy Spirit. The word used here for *temple* is a very special word. It is *naos*, which refers to the innermost sanctuary, the place of God's dwelling. It stands in contrast to the word *hieron*, which refers to the greater temple precincts as well as to the sanctuary. Just as the temple was the place to worship God, the church, as the temple of the Spirit, is to be a worshiping people.

The New Testament calls those who lead the church elders, bishops, or pastors; but they are never called priests. All believers are priests, and thus the doctrine of the priesthood of believers primarily designates believers' common responsibility to minister to one another and to the world.

Again, Hammett's summary helps us understand the church as the temple of the Holy Spirit:

1. Because it is God's holy temple, the church must be a worshiping community.
2. In God's temple all believers form the priesthood; all are involved in the church's ministry. We are all believer-priests.
3. The temple is also a place of relationship.
   - The Spirit mediates our relationship with God, communicating His presence and power and sanctifying us as we grow in Christlikeness.
   - The Spirit joins together believers as the living stones in God's temple through His creation of fellowship.[14]

Read the following Scripture passages and match each one with the biblical image to which it refers.

____ 1. 1 Corinthians 3:16		a.	The people of God
____ 2. 1 Peter 2:9		b.	The body of Christ
____ 3. 1 Corinthians 12:27		c.	The temple of the Holy Spirit

Match each statement to the biblical image of church to which it primarily refers.

_____ 1. All Christians are to be involved in ministry.

_____ 2. Christ is the ultimate authority for the church.

_____ 3. The church is connected to the redeemed in the Old Testament.

_____ 4. God took the initiative in calling a people to Himself.

_____ 5. The church must be a worshiping community.

_____ 6. Christ provides for the church's needs.

a. The people of God

b. The body of Christ

c. The temple of the Holy Spirit

Some of the statements can refer to more than one biblical image, but the most obvious answers are 1. c, 2. b, 3. a, 4. a, 5. c, 6. b.

A WORKING DEFINITION OF *CHURCH*

Baptists' strong interest in *ecclesiology*, or the doctrine of the church, has been a distinguishing characteristic since we began writing confessions nearly four hundred years ago.[15] Baptists were birthed from the free-church tradition. This means that Baptists rigorously seek to follow the New Testament in all it teaches and that Baptist churches are made up of baptized believers who operate through democratic processes under the spiritual leadership of pastors and deacons. Greg Wills points out that from their inception, "Baptist churches practiced a more thorough democracy than did the American federal and state governments."[16]

A brief survey of Baptist confessions of faith reveals Baptists' efforts to rigorously follow the New Testament teachings in their understanding of the church.

Compare and contrast the following four historical statements on the church.

Ecclesiology: the study of the church

The New Hampshire Confession, *1833*

OF A GOSPEL CHURCH

We believe that a visible Church of Christ is a congregation of baptized believers, associated by covenant in the faith and fellowship of the gospel; observing the ordinances of Christ; governed by his laws, and exercising the gifts, rights, and privileges invested in them by his Word; that its only scriptural officers are Bishops, or Pastors, and Deacons, whose qualifications, claims, and duties are defined in the Epistles to Timothy and Titus.

The Baptist Faith and Message, *1925*

THE GOSPEL CHURCH

A church of Christ is a congregation of baptized believers, associated by covenant in the faith and fellowship of the gospel; observing the ordinances of Christ, governed by his laws, and exercising the gifts, rights, and privileges invested in them by his word, and seeking to extend the gospel to the ends of the earth. Its Scriptural officers are bishops, or elders, and deacons. (Matt. 16:18; Matt. 18:15-18; Rom. 1:7; 1 Cor. 1:2; Acts 2:41-42; Acts 5:13-14; 2 Cor. 9:13; Phil. 1:1; 1 Tim. 4:14; Acts 14:23; Acts 6:3,5-6; Heb. 13:17; 1 Cor. 9:6,14)

"On this rock I will build My church, and the forces of Hades will not overpower it."

Matthew 16:18

The Baptist Faith and Message, *1963*

THE CHURCH

A New Testament church of the Lord Jesus Christ is a local body of baptized believers who are associated by covenant in the faith and fellowship of the gospel, observing the two ordinances of Christ, committed to His teachings, exercising the gifts, rights, and privileges invested in them by His Word, and seeking to extend the gospel to the ends of the earth.

This church is an autonomous body, operating through democratic processes under the Lordship of Jesus Christ. In such a congregation, members are equally responsible. Its Scriptural officers are pastors and deacons.

The New Testament speaks also of the church as the body of Christ which includes all of the redeemed of all the ages. (Matt. 16:15-19; 18:15-20; Acts 2:41-42,47; 5:11-14; 6:3-6; 13:1-3; 14:23,27; 15:1-30; 16:5; 20:28; Rom. 1:7; 1 Cor. 1:2; 3:16; 5:4-5; 7:17; 9:13-14; 12; Eph. 1:22-23; 2:19-22; 3:8-11,21; 5:22-32; Phil. 1:1; Col. 1:18; 1 Tim. 3:1-15; 4:14; 1 Pet. 5:1-4; Rev. 2–3; 21:2-3)

The Baptist Faith and Message, 2000

THE CHURCH

A New Testament church of the Lord Jesus Christ is an autonomous local congregation of baptized believers, associated by covenant in the faith and fellowship of the gospel; observing the two ordinances of Christ, governed by His laws, exercising the gifts, rights, and privileges invested in them by His Word, and seeking to extend the gospel to the ends of the earth. Each congregation operates under the Lordship of Christ through democratic processes. In such a congregation each member is responsible and accountable to Christ as Lord. Its scriptural officers are pastors and deacons. While both men and women are gifted for service in the church, the office of pastor is limited to men as qualified by Scripture.

> **A New Testament church of the Lord Jesus Christ is an autonomous local congregation of baptized believers.**

The New Testament speaks also of the church as the body of Christ which includes all of the redeemed of all the ages, believers from every tribe, and tongue, and people, and nation. (Matt. 16:15-19; 18:15-20; Acts 2:41-42,47; 5:11-14; 6:3-6; 13:1-3; 14:23,27; 15:1-30; 16:5; 20:28; Rom. 1:7; 1 Cor. 1:2; 3:16; 5:4-5; 7:17; 9:13-14; 12; Eph. 1:22-23; 2:19-22; 3:8-11,21; 5:22-32; Phil. 1:1; Col. 1:18; 1 Tim. 2:9-14; 3:1-15; 4:14; Heb. 11:39-40; 1 Pet. 5:1-4; Rev. 2–3; 21:2-3)

Let's compare some of the ways these confessions viewed the church.

The New Hampshire Confession (1833). This document speaks of the church as "a congregation of baptized believers, associated by covenant in the faith and fellowship of the Gospel. ... Officers are Bishops or

Pastors, and Deacons, whose qualifications, claims, and duties are defined in the Epistles to Timothy and Titus."[17]

The Baptist Faith and Message (1925). It is clear that the 1925 statement on the church is rooted in the *New Hampshire Confession,* with only minor changes. With respect to the offices of the church, scriptural officers are now "bishops, or *elders,* and deacons" (emphasis added). The *New Hampshire Confession* spoke of "Bishops or *Pastors,* and Deacons" (emphasis added). It is clear that the meaning of *elders* and *pastors* is the same.

The Baptist Faith and Message (1963). This revision of the 1925 statement significantly expanded the statement on the church. Added to the 1925 statement are emphases on—

- the local church and its autonomy;
- the fact that the congregation operates through democratic processes under the lordship of Jesus Christ;
- the equal responsibility of each member;
- the reality of the church as consisting of all the redeemed of all the ages.

Terms for the officers of the church are also changed in the 1963 statement. Now the officers are simply noted as being pastors and deacons. There is no reference to bishops or elders, in spite of their continuous presence in previous Baptist writings and confessions. However, we should probably not make too much out of this. It is likely that the 1963 confession simply represents the popular usage of the day; churches were now referring to their leaders as pastors. It is possible that the term *bishop* was now more easily misunderstood or even viewed negatively in the context of a growing Roman Catholic population in America.

The Baptist Faith and Message (2000). This confession is something of a theological landmark in the context of the theological controversy that shaped the Southern Baptist Convention in the 1980s and 1990s. The statement on the church is again similar to the 1925 and 1963 *Baptist Faith and Message* statements, but there are some important differences as well. The word *autonomous* has been moved toward the front of the article; and interestingly, the statement "operates under the lordship of Jesus Christ through democratic processes" reverses the order of the 1963 statement. This revision is more biblical in its order and also draws attention to the fact that we make our decisions and exercise our responsibility in relation to the lordship of Christ.

We make our decisions and exercise our responsibility in relation to the lordship of Christ.

Mark Dever is correct when he writes, "A church is not just straight-forward democracy, for in the churches there is a common recognition of our fallen state, of our tendency to err, and, on the other hand, of the inerrancy of God's Word. So the members of a church congregation are democratic, perhaps, only in the sense that they work together as a congregation to try to understand God's word. … As leaders and congregation, we strive for the unity of the Spirit in the bond of peace; we work together for what we believe would be best for the church."[18]

The 2000 statement on the church, like the 1963 statement, affirms the scriptural offices as pastors and deacons. Finally, the statement affirms all believers' gifts for service in the body of Christ but limits the office of pastor to men who are scripturally qualified.

In this brief survey one thing seems clear: Baptists have struggled—not always with success, to be sure—to remain faithful to the teachings of the New Testament in all matters of faith and practice. This dogged devotion to Scripture is also seen in their understanding of church government and polity.

For the purpose of this study, we will utilize article 6 of *The Baptist Faith and Message* (2000) as a working definition of *church*. This excellent statement is short and concise, biblical and practical. It sets reasonable parameters for like-minded brothers and sisters committed to the lordship of Christ and the authority of Scripture, but it does not dictate issues of methodology and practice that the Bible does not address. This statement provides Baptist churches a foundation for a diversity of methods that are grounded in biblical and theological unity.

Certainly Baptists, like others, have sometimes been captive to the currents of the culture that surrounds them. In recent years, however, Southern Baptists have swum against the currents of modernity and many other denominations. Their positions on issues like biblical inerrancy, abortion, homosexuality, the exclusivity of the gospel, and women as pastors are just a few examples. In the context of their polity, Southern Baptist churches have been fiercely congregational. They have consistently recognized only two offices in the local church—pastors and deacons. This is what the New Testament teaches. This is what Baptists seek to practice.

Baptists have struggled to remain faithful to the teachings of the New Testament in all matters of faith and practice.

PUTTING IT ALL TOGETHER

"I didn't realize there so many ideas about what a church is," Mark admitted to Jim. "I can see how we can get in trouble in our churches today. We had a big fight in our church three years ago over a building program. I think some of us thought the building was the church, as if we were more concerned about bricks and wood than people."

Jim responded, "This was a lot of information about what a church is. Let me see if I can go to the definition of the 2000 *Baptist Faith and Message* to get it clear." Jim got a piece of paper and began to list the characteristics of a church:

- The church is an autonomous and local congregation.
- The church consists of baptized believers.
- The church is associated by covenant in the faith and fellowship of the gospel.
- The church observes two ordinances.
- The church is governed by Christ's laws.
- In the church, believers exercise the gifts, rights, and privileges invested in them by God's Word.
- The church seeks to extend the gospel to the ends of the earth.
- The church operates under the lordship of Christ through democratic processes.
- Each church member is responsible and accountable to Christ as Lord.
- The scriptural officers of the church are pastors and deacons.
- The office of pastor is limited to men, as qualified by Scripture.

In the church, believers exercise the gifts, rights, and privileges invested in them by God's Word.

"This list helps define *church*," Jim said to Mark, but I'm really curious as to whether we would recognize a church today as a true New Testament church by visiting it for a few weeks. I really wonder whether we could tell that a particular church is acting like a church."

"I think you just sent us on another study," Mark laughed. "Now we have to spend some time looking for the marks of a true church."

We will join Jim and Mark's search in chapter 2.

Refer to the definition of *church* you wrote on page 12. In light of what you have learned from this chapter, rewrite your definition here.

_____

_____

_____

_____

_____

_____

_____

🔍 Review your memory verse for this chapter.

🔍 Close your study by thanking God for choosing you to be a member of His church—the local church to which you belong and the redeemed of all the ages.

LEADER GUIDE

JUST WHAT IS THE CHURCH ANYWAY?

BEFORE THE SESSION

1. Study chapter 1 and complete the learning activities.
2. Write the following Scripture references on separate index cards: *Romans 12:4-5; 1 Corinthians 3:16; 1 Corinthians 6:19; 1 Corinthians 12:27; 1 Peter 2:9.*
3. Have available large sheets of paper and felt-tip pens.

DURING THE SESSION

1. Greet everyone, make needed introductions, and help everyone feel at ease. Make sure everyone has a copy of the book.
2. Distribute large sheets of paper and felt-tip pens and ask members to work in pairs to make a drawing of the church. Do not elaborate on what you mean by the word *church*. Allow a few minutes for the activity. Then mount the drawings at the front of the room. Do not comment on the drawings or ask members to interpret them until later in the session.
3. Share that the topic for this study is vibrant church. Ask: *What does the word* vibrant *mean?* Write responses on a dry-erase board. State that the word as used in this study means *healthy.* Referring to page 8, overview the six chapters of the study. Share the four suggested goals for the study from page 9.
4. Ask volunteers to share their earliest memories of church.
5. Ask members to work in the same pairs again to write a definition of *church.* As the definitions are shared, it will be obvious that multiple usages of the term abound.
6. Share the background and meaning of the word *ekklesia* from pages 15–17, including the four uses of the word in the New Testament: a local church, a house church, a collection of churches, and the universal church.
7. Call attention to members' drawings of the church that are displayed on the wall. Using the section "Correctives in Defining *Church*," beginning on page 18, point out contemporary uses of the word. Ask members to evaluate whether each drawing reflects a correct or an incorrect idea of what the church is.

8. Refer to the activity on page 19. As you read each statement, ask members to decide whether it refers to the primary meaning of *church* in the New Testament (a local body of believers).

9. Point out that the New Testament writers used a number of images for church. Write on a dry-erase board the headings *People of God, Body of Christ*, and *Temple of the Holy Spirit* and point out that these are three prominent images. Divide members into five groups and distribute the index cards with Scripture references. Ask the groups to read the Scriptures and to identify which New Testament image of the church is described.

10. Point to the heading *People of God* on the board. Use the material on page 20 to explain how the image *people of God* connects the church to the Israelites in the Old Testament. Ask: *What are some practical implications of the term* people of God *for the church?* Point to the heading *Body of Christ* on the board. Ask: *How does this image highlight unity? How does this image emphasize unity in diversity? What does the image imply about love and care in the church? Who is the head of the church? What are some implications for the church since Christ is the head of the body?* Point to the heading *Temple of the Holy Spirit* on the board. Ask: *What does this image imply about the church's worship? What are some practical implications for a believer's daily living? What kind of sacrifice should a Christian make to God (see Rom. 12:1)?*

11. Call attention to the *Baptist Faith and Message* (2000) statement on page 27. Ask members to name all the points or statements they can find about the basic nature and essence of the church as you write them on a dry-erase board. Refer to the summary list on page 30 and ask members to identify any ideas that are not on the board. Allow time for discussion of and questions about the statements.

12. Ask volunteers to share how they would change the definitions of *church* they wrote at the beginning of the session.

13. Call attention to this week's memory verse, 1 Peter 2:9. Lead the group in reading the verse aloud several times. Encourage members to commit to memorize the verse.

14. State that our English word *church* comes from the Greek word *kuriakon*. Write the two words on a dry-erase board. Explain that the meaning of the Greek word is *belonging to the Lord*. Ask members to bow their heads and close their eyes for prayer. Say: *Think not only about our church as belonging to the Lord but also about your life as belonging to the Lord. Meditate on the following questions.* Read the questions in the activity on pages 13–14. Close with a prayer of thanksgiving that God has chosen us to be members of His church, both the local church and the redeemed of all ages. Ask God to help each member and your church to more completely surrender to and serve the head of the church, Jesus Christ.

15. Ask members to read chapter 2 and to complete the activities before the next session.

Chapter 2

IS MY CHURCH ACTING LIKE THE CHURCH?

⚠ Learning Goal

A study of this chapter will help you gain a better understanding of the essential marks or distinctives of a New Testament church.

🔥 Memory Verses

"There is one body and one Spirit, just as you were called to one hope at your calling; one Lord, one faith, one baptism, one God and Father of all, who is above all and through all and in all" (Eph. 4:4-6).

What are the marks of a New Testament church? What are the marks of a healthy church? These related questions are theological and practical, biblical and historical. This chapter builds on our study in chapter 1, in which we examined the *nature* of the church. Now we will identify the *marks* of the church. In chapter 5 we will see how all this comes together in the *mission* of the church. But let's not get ahead of ourselves. What are the essential, nonnegotiable evidences of a New Testament church? With that question in mind, we return to Mark and Jim's discussion.

"I think one of the reasons people like me don't attend church is that we don't really think the church is important to our lives," Jim said.

"Why is that?" Mark responded. "Why don't you think the church is important to your life?"

Jim paused for a moment and then responded, "To be honest, I sometimes have trouble seeing the difference between churches I've attended and the country club or civic club where I'm a member. Sure, the churches have more religious language than the country club, but the members seem to act about the same. Both sets of members seem to be there for the fellowship and for the benefits they get. I guess I sound cynical, but I haven't seen much reason to attend church when I get better benefits from the country club."

Mark was at first taken aback by Jim's comments. But he realized that Jim's honesty reflected a reality that could not be missed. Many people, even church members, see little difference between their churches and other organizations.

"You're right, Jim, and you're not alone," Mark sighed. "I just read that in the Southern Baptist Convention fewer than half of our members attend on a given Sunday. We have more than 16 million members, but only 7 million are in worship services each week. Obviously, our own members don't see church as important to their lives, so I can see why unchurched people like you feel the same way."

The two men had earlier decided to study how the church is supposed to look and act. But this discussion made them even more eager to continue their study. As they had done in their study of the nature and the essence of the church, they borrowed books and checked out others from a local seminary library. In their quest to find the vibrant church, they were curious to see both the biblical background and the historical record of what a true New Testament church looks like.

THE HISTORICAL RECORD

The Christian church now has two thousand years of recorded history. As you might expect, many changes have taken place throughout this time; yet some characteristics of the church remain much the same and are as relevant in churches today as they were in the early years of the church. Let's look at biblical marks of the church that have endured over time.

THE EARLY CHURCH

When the Council of Constantinople came together in A.D. 381 to address a heresy about Jesus, it also spoke to the issue of ecclesiology, stating that Christians "believe in one holy, catholic and apostolic church."[1] The four adjectives describe four key marks of a New Testament church.

> Circle the four words that describe the church in the council's statement above.

"*The multitude of those who believed were of one heart and soul, and no one said that any of his possessions was his own, but instead they held everything in common.*"

Acts 4:32

The Council of Constantinople: The church is—

- one;
- holy;
- universal;
- apostolic.

The church is one. The church is one just as God is one. The church as the body of the one Lord Jesus Christ is to be known for its oneness, or unity. Christians should be characterized by their unity (see Acts 4:32). Believers' unity is to be evident in the church and as a witness to the world. Divisions and disputes bring shame to the church and harm its testimony.

Scripture repeatedly affirms the oneness of the body of Christ. In Ephesians Paul wrote, "There is one body and one Spirit, just as you were called to one hope at your calling; one Lord, one faith, one baptism, one God and Father of all, who is above all and through all and in all" (Eph. 4:4-6). Mark Dever notes, "In 1 Corinthians 1, Paul argued for the unity of the Christians based on their unity in Christ. In Romans 12 and 1 Corinthians 12, Paul taught there is one body. And in Galatians 3:27-28, Paul said that Christians are all one in Christ, regardless of ethnicity. Paul's teaching reflects Christ's own teaching that there is one flock (John 10:16). So Christ prayed in John 17:21 for his followers to be one."[2]

The church's unity is a spiritual reality, "consisting in the fellowship of all true believers sharing in the Holy Spirit. It becomes visible when believers share the same baptism, partake of the same supper, and look forward to sharing one heavenly city. The church on earth experiences this unity only as they are united in God's truth as it is revealed in Scripture."[3]

Describe one of the most meaningful things to you about your church's fellowship and unity.

_____

_____

State one action you can take to promote the unity and fellowship of your church.

_____

_____

The church is holy. The church is to be holy because God is holy (see Lev. 11:44-45; 19:2; 20:7; 1 Pet. 1:14-16). As the dwelling place of the Holy Spirit, the church is made up of saints set apart for God (see 1 Cor. 1:2). Our holiness is at the most basic level Christ's holiness; His holiness should be reflected in the church's holiness (see Rom. 6:14; Phil. 3:8-9). In the beautiful Ephesians text Paul wrote that "Christ loved the church and gave himself for her, to make her holy, cleansing her in the washing of water by the word. He did this to present the church to Himself in splendor, without spot or wrinkle or any such thing, but holy and blameless" (Eph. 5:25-27).

"As obedient children, do not be conformed to the desires of your former ignorance but, as the One who called you is holy, you also are to be holy in all your conduct; for it is written, 'Be holy, because I am holy.'"

1 Peter 1:14-16

Read each Scripture passage and match it with the correct summary statement.

___ 1. Leviticus 19:2

___ 2. Isaiah 6:1-5

___ 3. Romans 6:14

___ 4. 1 Corinthians 1:2

___ 5. Ephesians 5:25-27

___ 6. Philippians 3:8-9

___ 7. 1 Thessalonians 4:3

a. Our sanctification is God's will for us.

b. Awareness of God's holiness makes us realize our uncleanness.

c. Our righteousness is inadequate; we have righteousness from God.

d. We should be holy because God is holy.

e. Christians are called saints.

f. Christ loved the church and gave Himself to make it holy.

g. Christians should not be mastered by sin.

Answers: 1. d, 2. b, 3. g, 4. e, 5. f, 6. c, 7. a

In this present age the church will never attain perfect experiential holiness. John Calvin put it well in this summarization: the Lord is daily at work in smoothing out wrinkles and cleansing spots. From this it follows that the church's holiness is not yet complete. The church is holy, then, in the sense that it is daily advancing and is not yet perfect.[4]

Name two ways God is at work in smoothing out wrinkles and cleansing spots in your life.

1. _____

2. _____

The church is universal. The church is universal because it spans space and time. Dever notes, "*Catholic* is the older English word used to describe this attribute. But because of that word's association with the Church of Rome, *universality* provides a better translation of the Greek word originally used in the creeds, *katholicain*."[5] Universality is not the domain of any one group of true Christians. Ignatius of Antioch wrote in the early second century that "where Jesus Christ is there is the universal church."[6]

While every true local church is part of this universal church and is a church in and of itself, no local church can be said to constitute the universal church. However, the church in both its local and universal manifestations is the body of Christ and is to reflect and honor Him.

The church is apostolic. The church is *apostolic* because it is founded on the Scriptures given through the apostles. The gospel and "the faith that was delivered to the saints once for all" (Jude 3) have been passed down from the apostles who were called to be with Jesus. In that sense, a succession of apostolic teaching, based on the Word of God, has come down through the ages. Paul told the church at Ephesus that it had been "built on the foundation of the apostles and prophets, with Christ Jesus Himself as the chief cornerstone" (Eph. 2:20). Dever notes, "The succession that followed the setting of this foundation may not always have involved a person-to-person transmission, but there has been a succession of faithful teaching of the truth."[7] Thus, the continuity between the teaching in churches today and the teaching of the apostles is absolutely necessary for the constitution and expression of a true church. "Only with the apostles' teaching is the church, as Paul described it to Timothy, 'the pillar and foundation of the truth' (1 Tim. 3:15)."[8]

Catholic:

universal

Apostolic:

founded on the Scriptures given through the apostles

Read each Scripture passage and match it with the correct affirmation about the church.

____ 1. Romans 12:1-2   a. The church is one.

____ 2. Romans 12:4-5   b. The church is holy.

____ 3. Ephesians 1:22-23   c. The church is universal.

____ 4. Ephesians 2:18-22   d. The church is apostolic.

Answers: 1. b,

2. a, 3. c, 4. d

Mark each statement *T* (true) or *F* (false).

____ 1. A Christian can achieve perfect holiness in this life.

____ 2. God used the apostles to build the church.

____ 3. The church of Jesus Christ spans space and time.

____ 4. A church witnesses to the world through its love and unity.

____ 5. The local church and the universal church are one and the same.

____ 6. God does not expect Christians to be holy.

True: 2, 3, 4

False: 1, 5, 6

CONTRIBUTIONS FROM THE REFORMATION

The Protestant Reformation of the 16th century shattered and divided the Roman Catholic Church. New questions were immediately raised as to what constitutes a true church. This question was not theoretical. It was crucially important as Protestants in particular sought an identity as a body of believers under the lordship of Jesus Christ.

The reformers (Luther, Calvin, and Zwingli), for the most part, agreed in their answers to the question "What constitutes a true church?" It was (1) the Word rightly preached and (2) the sacraments properly administered.

The Word rightly preached. Luther emphasized the Word of God. He argued that "even if there were no other sign than this alone, it would still suffice to prove that a Christian, holy people must exist there, for God's Word cannot be without God's people, and conversely, God's people cannot be without God's Word."[9] In one of his writings, Luther listed seven marks of a true church: (1) the Word, (2) baptism, (3) the Lord's Supper, (4) church discipline, (5) called and consecrated ministers, (6) public praise and thanksgiving, and (7) the sacred cross of suffering.[10]

The sacraments properly administered. Christian groups disagree about what this phrase means. Roman Catholics believe that the sacraments impart divine grace and therefore have the power to save. Churches

Reformers:

Luther, Zwingli, Calvin, and their followers

The Reformation:
• The Word rightly preached
• The sacraments properly administered

Ordinance:

decree or

command

of Christ view baptism as essential for salvation, even though they call baptism and the Lord's Supper ordinances, just as Baptists do. Baptists believe that the Lord's Supper and baptism are ordinances—prescribed practices or ceremonies—that Christians do as acts of obedience, symbolism, and remembrance. They are not sacraments because they are not necessary for salvation, and no divine act automatically occurs when people participate in these church practices.

Match each term with the correct definition.

___ 1. Ordinance

___ 2. Sacrament

a. A symbolic ceremony commanded by Christ

b. A ceremony believed to bestow divine grace to the recipient

Answers: 1. a, 2. b

Calvin is well known for his famous affirmation "Wherever the Word of God purely preached and heard, the sacraments are administered according to Christ's institution, a church of God undoubtedly exists."[11] Calvin, on occasion, also added church discipline as a third mark. Hammett provides a superb analysis of these Reformation emphases when he writes, "These signs [Word and sacraments] relate directly to the struggle the Reformers had with the Catholic Church. The identifying slogans of the Reformation (*sola Scriptura, sola gratia, sola fide* [Scripture alone, grace alone, faith alone]) are all encompassed in their marks."[12]

Without referring to the paragraph above, match each statement with the correct Latin phrase.

___ 1. Salvation is God's free gift made possible by Christ's death and resurrection rather than by human merit.

___ 2. Scripture alone is the source of Christian revelation.

___ 3. The only way to receive God's grace and be saved is through faith in Christ.

a. Sola Scriptura

b. Sola gratia

c. Sola fide

Answers: 1. b, 2. a, 3. c

REGENERATE CHURCH MEMBERSHIP:
A BAPTIST DISTINCTIVE

Anabaptists and Baptists went further than the reformers when they insisted on a believers' church. They more truly followed to its logical end a return to *sola Scriptura* (Scripture alone) and the New Testament pattern for the church. The conclusion they reached was inescapable: the church is to be composed of regenerate members—those who are true believers in Jesus Christ. J. D. Freeman would state at the first Baptist World Congress in 1905, "This principle of a regenerated church membership, more than anything else, marks our distinctiveness in the Christian world today."[12]

Regenerate: having experienced the new birth—God's work in the new believer at conversion to create a new person empowered by the Holy Spirit

The biblical basis for a regenerate church is clear. Hammett provides four strong arguments to support the essential nature of this doctrine.

1. It is a matter of logic. If the universal church is composed of believers, the goal of local churches should be the same.

2. The New Testament anticipates the possibility that local churches will unintentionally allow false members to come in (see 2 Pet. 2:1; Jude 4), and it provides a means to address the issue—church discipline (see 1 Cor. 5).

3. The descriptions of local churches in the New Testament assume that these congregations are composed of believers only. Hammett writes, "The church of God in Corinth is called 'those sanctified in Christ Jesus' (1 Cor. 1:2). The letter to the Ephesians is addressed to 'the saints in Ephesus, the faithful in Christ Jesus' (Eph. 1:1). The letter to the church in Philippi is sent 'to all the saints in Christ Jesus' (Phil. 1:1). Paul wrote 'to the holy and faithful brothers in Christ at Colosse' (Col. 1:2). The church of the Thessalonians is described in both letters as a church 'in God the Father and the Lord Jesus Christ' (1 Thess. 1:1; 2 Thess. 1:2). Clearly, Paul thought he was addressing bodies of Christians."

4. Local churches in Acts were composed of only those who believed. The church in Jerusalem is identified as those who "accepted his [Peter's] message" (Acts 2:41). Those who were added in later days were those "who were being saved" (Acts 2:47), or those who heard the message of the gospel and believed (see Acts 4:4). "The clear implication is that those churches were composed of believers. ... Paul's regular strategy was to enter a city, preach the gospel, and organize those who responded into churches. He operated with the assumption of regenerate church membership."[14]

Suppose a fellow church member asked you, "Why does our church insist that only believers can belong? I think our church should be open to anyone who wants to become a member." How would you respond?

AN ASSESSMENT OF THE MARKS OF A NEW TESTAMENT CHURCH

A New Testament church is identified by particular distinctives. Baptists, in particular, have sought to find and establish their identity and practice in the New Testament. A survey of the New Testament will reveal some nonnegotiable building blocks of the church. What must our churches look like if they are to resemble those of our first-century forefathers? We will highlight seven essential characteristics.

REGENERATE CHURCH MEMBERSHIP

Marks of a New Testament church:

- **Regenerate church membership**
- **Ordinances**
- **Church discipline**
- **Word-based ministry**
- **Biblical ecclesiology of leadership and governance**
- **Missions and evangelism**
- **Sound theology**

A regenerate church has always characterized a true church. The membership of a local church is made up of those who repent of sin and confess Christ as Savior and Lord. As noted earlier, this principle set Baptists apart from the reformers, but they adopted this position because of their commitment to the witness of the New Testament. There is no hint whatsoever of unregenerate church membership in the Bible, although the unregenerate are often present among the people of God. The apostle John acknowledged in 1 John 2:19, "They went out from us, but they did not belong to us; for if they had belonged to us, they would have remained with us. However, they went out so that it might be made clear that none of them belongs to us."

The failure to uphold this principle with the most fervent commitment has always hurt the church. Stan Norman is correct when he notes, "Failing to emphasize regeneration as a prerequisite for church membership has historically resulted in the loss of an emphasis upon the church as a holy community and has given rise to moral corruption and heretical teaching within the fellowship."[15]

A New Testament church makes it clear that church membership is a privilege and a responsibility, not a right. Requirements and expectations for local-church membership must be clearly defined and articulated. This involves more than raising a hand, walking an aisle, or filling out a card. It requires an understanding of the gospel; public confession of one's faith, evidenced by a clear verbal testimony and water baptism; and a pledge to walk in the newness of life in Christ. Churches must also be careful to avoid practicing early-adolescent baptism that lacks a clear understanding and confession of the gospel. The large numbers of rebaptisms today must give us pause. The same is true of inflated membership rolls filled with the names of persons who now give little or no evidence of faith.

Further, a New Testament church guards against "easy believism" and a compromised gospel. The gracious invitation to believe in Christ must be complemented by the call to repent of sin. To omit repentance is to preach only half the gospel. It is to ignore the first public preaching of John the Baptist (see Matt. 3:1-2), Jesus (see Matt. 4:17), and Peter (see Acts 2:38). It is to neglect the missionary proclamation replete in the Book of Acts, in which persons are called to turn in "repentance toward God and faith in our Lord Jesus" (Acts 20:21). Maintaining the nonnegotiable of a regenerate church demands effective evangelism and discipleship at every level of church life.

> **The gracious invitation to believe in Christ must be complemented by the call to repent of sin.**

Identify ways your church receives persons for membership.

THE ORDINANCES: BAPTISM AND THE LORD'S SUPPER

Baptism and the Lord's Supper are practiced today, much as they have been throughout the history of the church, as two signs of Jesus' presence, given by Christ Himself. First, Jesus asked John the Baptist to baptize Him even though He had no need; being sinless, He had no reason to confess or repent. His action, however, gave believers an example to follow.

Jesus also instituted the Lord's Supper with His disciples during Passover, saying as He broke the bread, "This is My body, which is given for you. Do this in remembrance of Me." Later He said as He "took the cup after supper, 'This cup is the new covenant established by My blood; it is shed for you' " (Luke 22:19-21).

Mark each statement *A* (agree) or *D* (disagree).

_____ 1. Every new believer should be baptized.

_____ 2. Baptism is optional for a believer.

_____ 3. Baptism has saving merit.

_____ 4. Sprinkling is an acceptable form of baptism.

_____ 5. Baptism symbolizes a believer's faith in a crucified, buried, and risen Savior.

_____ 6. Baptism completes salvation.

Check your answers as you continue reading. We agree with statements 1 and 5. We disagree with 2, 3, 4, and 6.

Believer's baptism by immersion. In the New Testament public confession of Jesus Christ as Savior and Lord was not demonstrated by walking an aisle to the front of the meeting room at the time of invitation. Public confession in Christ was by baptism. Indeed, an "unbaptized believer" is an anomaly in light of the New Testament. Closely connected to but distinct from regeneration/conversion,[16] baptism is the means by which someone publicly declares faith in Jesus Christ for salvation and is initiated into the believing community.[17]

Explain in your own words the following statement: "An 'unbaptized believer' is an anomaly in light of the New Testament."

_____

_____

The belief that baptism involves a believer baptized by immersion as a public identification with Christ and the believing community is grounded in the New Testament witness and has been a hallmark of Baptists throughout their history. To be a Baptist is to champion believer's baptism by immersion. Baptists have chosen to remain faithful to the meaning of the word *baptism*, taken from the Greek word *baptizo*, which means *immerse*. *The Baptist Faith and Message* (2000) says it well: "Christian baptism is the immersion of a believer in water in the name of the Father, the Son, and the Holy Spirit. It is an act of obedience symbolizing the believer's faith in a crucified, buried, and risen Savior, the believer's death to sin, the burial of the old life, and the resurrection to walk in newness of life in Christ Jesus. It is a testimony to his faith in the final resurrection of the dead. Being a church ordinance, it is prerequisite to the privileges of church membership and to the Lord's Supper."[18]

We must see evidence of regeneration in those we baptize. Baptism of young children must be administered with the greatest possible care. Baptism should be viewed and emphasized as a first and necessary step of discipleship and obedience to Christ; therefore, we must reject as inconceivable the idea of admitting anyone into our membership without believer's baptism by immersion.

The issue here is obedience. In churches today, when people make the decision to accept Christ as Savior and follow Him as Lord, they are said to make a public profession of faith. Some people have come to understand that public profession as walking down the aisle, though this is not the current practice in all churches. But the public profession of belief in Christ is actually baptism, a believer's first act of obedience to his Lord. How can someone say he has made the decision to follow Christ and then refuse to be baptized? All believers should take this first step of obedience, symbolizing the death and burial of their old lives and their resurrection into new life in Christ.

Check the response that best completes the following sentence. Baptism symbolizes—
○ 1. a believer's faith in a crucified, buried, and risen Savior;
○ 2. a believer's death to sin, burial of the old life, and resurrection to walk in newness of life in Christ Jesus;
○ 3. a believer's faith in the final resurrection of the dead;
○ 4. all of the above.

> Baptism symbolizes all of these.

Mark each statement A (agree) or D (disagree).
___ 1. The Lord's Supper was begun by the early church.
___ 2. The Lord's Supper is one way to proclaim the Lord's death.
___ 3. The Lord's Supper is for everyone, Christians and non-Christians alike.
___ 4. The Lord's Supper is a symbolic act of obedience that imparts divine grace to a believer.
___ 5. A person should examine his life and repent of all sin before taking part in the Lord's Supper.
___ 6. The Lord's Supper symbolizes Christ's atoning work.

> Check your work as you continue reading. We agree with statements 2, 5, and 6. We disagree with 1, 3, and 4.

The Lord's Supper. Christians celebrate this ordinance to memorialize Jesus for His sacrificial death while also anticipating His coming again. It is a symbolic act of obedience for those who call Him Savior and Lord. Although only Luke among the Gospels specifically quotes Jesus as saying, "Do this in remembrance of Me" (Luke 22:19), Matthew 26:26-30 and Mark 14:22-26 also describe the Supper.

Paul's writings indicate that the early church practiced the Lord's Supper: "The cup of blessing that we bless, is it not a sharing in the blood of Christ? The bread that we break, is it not a sharing in the body of Christ? Because there is one bread, we who are many are one body, for all of us share that one bread" (1 Cor. 10:16-17). Later in 1 Corinthians Paul wrote, "I received from the Lord what I also passed on to you: on the night when He was betrayed, the Lord Jesus took bread, gave thanks, broke it, and said, 'This is My body, which is for you. Do this in remembrance of Me.' In the same way He also took the cup, after supper, and said, 'This cup is the new covenant in My blood. Do this, as often as you drink it, in remembrance of Me.' For as often as you eat this bread and drink the cup, you proclaim the Lord's death until He comes. Therefore, whoever eats the bread or drinks the cup of the Lord in an unworthy way will be guilty of sin against the body and blood of the Lord. So a man should examine himself; in this way he should eat of the bread and drink of the cup" (1 Cor. 11:23-28).

From these verses we can see that the Lord's Supper is to be celebrated by the church, one body of Christ united in Him. The ordinance looks back to Jesus' death and forward to His coming again. It is to be celebrated by people who are in a right relationship with God—those who are regenerate, have examined their lives, have repented of their sin, and seek to live in fellowship with God and with their brothers in sisters in a particular body of Christ.

> **The Lord's Supper is to be celebrated by the church, one body of Christ united in Him.**

Paul's descriptions of the practice in his day are the model for celebrating the Lord's Supper in churches today. The Bible doesn't tell us how often to celebrate the Lord's Supper. Jesus said, "Do this in remembrance of Me" (Luke 22:19). Paul wrote, "As often as you eat this bread and drink the cup …" (1 Cor. 11:26). Most Baptist churches do not celebrate the Lord's Supper every week so that it doesn't become a meaningless ritual. However, they celebrate it on a regular frequency, usually somewhere between monthly and quarterly, so that they regularly obey Christ's command to observe this memorial and keep its meaning fresh. To be faithful, we will continue this celebration until Christ returns.

Complete the following sentences.

The Lord's Supper looks back to _____.

The Lord's Supper looks forward to _____.

What is most meaningful to you about observing the Lord's Supper?

_____

_____

CHURCH DISCIPLINE

Because of the importance of this doctrine, we will dedicate a full chapter to it. Here we will only briefly summarize its importance.

The New Testament clearly and repeatedly teaches church discipline. Jesus addressed it in Matthew 18:15-20, and Paul did so in 1 Corinthians 5:1-13; 2 Corinthians 2:5-11; Galatians 6:1-4; and Titus 3:9-11. Historically, Baptists have viewed church discipline as an essential mark of the church, along with the Word rightly preached and the ordinances properly administered. We find this fact evidenced in our earliest confessions, going back to the Anabaptists. Anabaptism was known for its emphasis on church discipline, beginning with the Schleitheim Confession of 1527. Article 2 on the ban states, "Second. We are agreed as follows on the ban. The ban shall be employed with all those who have given themselves to the Lord, to walk in His commandments, and with all those who are baptized into the one body of Christ and who are called brethren or sisters and yet who slip sometimes and fall into error and sin, being inadvertently overtaken. The same shall be admonished twice in secret and the third time openly disciplined or banned according to the command of Christ. Matt. 18. But this shall be done according to the regulation of the Spirit (Matt. 5) before the breaking of bread, so that we may break and eat one bread, with one mind and in love and may drink of one cup."[19]

"Avoid foolish debates, genealogies, quarrels, and disputes about the law, for they are unprofitable and worthless. Reject a divisive person after a first and second warning, knowing that such a person is perverted and sins, being self-condemned."

Titus 3:9-11

We must teach church members what the Bible says about church discipline. They must see its biblical basis and its spiritual necessity. Further, we must begin to implement church discipline lovingly and wisely. Finally, we must apply discipline to the specific sins Paul listed in 1 Corinthians 5. This list is not exhaustive, but it is a proper place to begin and a proper guide to direct us. Church discipline is not an optional mark but a desperately essential one.

A WORD-BASED MINISTRY

We live in a day when the words of the prophet Amos have never been more true. In many of our Baptist churches, there is

> a famine through the land:
> not a famine of food or a thirst for water,
> but a famine of hearing the words of the LORD (Amos 8:11).

Stephen Prothero, a teacher at Boston College, has referred to America as "a nation of religious illiterates." Writing for the *Los Angeles Times*, he noted that Americans claim to be religious, and the most popular religion is Christianity. Europeans are much less likely to believe in miracles, hell, or biblical inerrancy; but they know far more about the Bible and about religion than Americans do. In Europe schoolchildren learn about religion, beginning in the elementary years in school. Apparently, Americans don't learn about it anywhere. Few can even name the four Gospels or tell you what the Bible says about any given subject, such as homosexuality or abortion.[20]

The fault lies with the churches. In an attempt to be popular and relevant, many churches have become foolish and irrelevant. Skiing across the surface needs of a fallen, sinful humanity, they have turned to teaching and preaching pop-psychology sideshows and offering feel-good pit stops. They have neglected preaching and teaching the whole counsel of God's Word and the theology of God's Word. Too many of our people know neither the content nor the doctrines of Scripture. Some pastors and teachers choose to focus on politics; others, the emotions; still others, relationships; and the list goes on and on. If they use the Bible at all, it is usually as a proof text out of context, with no real connection to its intended meaning.

Too many of our people know neither the content nor the doctrines of Scripture.

For those of us who profess to believe both the inerrancy and sufficiency of Scripture, we must return to preaching and teaching that are biblical in content. There must be engaging exposition in our pulpits that is dynamic in delivery. Transformational preaching is expositional and theological on the one hand and practical and applicable on the other. Such preaching models the way people should teach the Bible.

What are two forms of evidence that your church practices a Word-based ministry?

1. _____

2. _____

A BIBLICAL ECCLESIOLOGY OF LEADERSHIP AND GOVERNANCE

The doctrine of the church has become a point of significant debate, especially in terms of polity, or church governance. Because of its importance, we will also dedicate a full chapter to this subject as well. Here we will make a few important observations in the context of the essential marks of a church.

Polity: church governance

Congregationalism: a form of church government holding that the authority of the church resides in each local body of believers

Article 6 on the church in *The Baptist Faith and Message* (2000) speaks to the issue of church governance: "Each congregation operates under the Lordship of Christ through democratic processes. In such a congregation each member is responsible and accountable to Christ as Lord. Its scriptural officers are pastors and deacons. While both men and women are gifted for service in the church, the office of pastor is limited to men as qualified by Scripture."[21]

Scripture does not set forth the specifics of congregationalism, though congregationalism in some form is clearly the most defensible form of church government, based on the New Testament. The concept that every member is a minister is biblical and essential. At the same time, capable, trusted church leadership is a must if members are to be equipped to minister effectively.

Leaders in Baptist churches have traditionally been pastors and deacons, the two scriptural officers described in the New Testament. As churches have grown, ministers and support personnel have been added.

Today books are exploring the nature of church government and the nature of church offices in terms of function and number, particularly that of the pastor, or elder.[22] It is interesting to note that throughout Baptist history our confessions, until recently, favored the terms *bishops* and *elders*. Part of the current debate is over which term to use, *pastor* or *elder*. There has also been debate about a plurality of spiritual leaders versus a single pastor.[23] Neither Scripture nor Baptist confessions specify the number of pastors/elders, though they are almost always referred to in the plural. However, there is no debate that a properly constituted church will have both a pastor and deacons. We will deal more with this debate in the next chapter.

State two forms of evidence that your church practices congregational church government.

1. _____

2. _____

MISSIONS AND EVANGELISM

Southern Baptists are known for missions and evangelism. In so many ways these tasks define who we are. Jimmy Draper has well said, "Evangelism and missions. Those things are in our DNA." However, recent trends in Southern Baptist baptisms have not been promising. Draper provides an analysis, noting, "Unfortunately we as a denomination and as churches have strayed somewhat from that [evangelism and missions] foundation, often focusing on a lot of things that have nothing to do with either of those."[24]

"Keep a clear head about everything, endure hardship, do the work of an evangelist, fulfill your ministry."

2 Timothy 4:5

In our three decades of ministry, we have become absolutely convinced of an unquestionable truth: *no church will be evangelistic by accident.* Churches naturally do some things well with ease because of their interest, context, and membership; but no church is inclined to do evangelism. It must be intentional, it must be a priority, and it must start with church leaders. Pastors are called to do the work of an evangelist, according to 2 Timothy 4:5. They must set the pace for the rest of the congregation.

Churches can carry out missions and evangelism in numerous ways. Here are some basic ideas.

Wed evangelism to sound biblical doctrine. For church members to embrace the importance of missions and evangelism, we need to teach and nurture a healthy understanding of related biblical doctrines, such as God's sovereignty and human responsibility, the danger of inclusivism (believing that Jesus will save followers of false religions), and the doctrine of the Holy Spirit. Evangelism, joined to balanced biblical theology, will go far in equipping churches to move out in obedience to fulfill the Great Commission of our Lord (see Matt. 28:18-20).

Train church members as personal evangelists. Churches can train personal evangelists by using resources like *FAITH Evangelism* and *Share Jesus Without Fear*. Choose a witnessing strategy that works best with your church and in your setting; the important thing is to equip church members to share the gospel of Jesus wherever they go.

Use a multifaceted approach. Methods can be created and adapted to share the timeless truth of the gospel in a changing society. Marketplace evangelism in the workplace is an area that needs attention, strategizing, and training. Youth and student evangelism needs renewed emphasis.

Take the gospel to ethnic groups. Challenge members to reach out to the exploding ethnic and minority groups across America. Because the authenticity and integrity of the gospel are at stake, bigotry and prejudice must be confronted for the ugly sins they are. God has brought a mission field to our land. If we ignore it, He will certainly and rightly judge us.

Whatever evangelistic methods are used, the key is to act. We can train and we can preach on evangelism, but we must also *do* it. Genuine, biblical evangelism must be a constant drumbeat in a vibrant New Testament church.

Name two ways your church is involved in evangelism.

1. _____

2. _____

Describe two ways your church is involved in missions.

1. _____

2. _____

"Jesus came near and said to them, 'All authority has been given to Me in heaven and on earth. Go, therefore, and make disciples of all nations, baptizing them in the name of the Father and of the Son and of the Holy Spirit, teaching them to observe everything I have commanded you. And remember, I am with you always, to the end of the age.' "

Matthew 28:18-20

SOUND THEOLOGY

Biblical theology is a mark of a healthy church. God intends for His church to be a theological academy. Theology allows us to glorify God with our minds and obey Jesus' command to "love the Lord your God with all your heart, with all your soul, and with all your mind" (Matt. 22:37).

This was the vision of our founding father of theological education, James Petigru Boyce (1827–88). His inaugural address, delivered as a professor of theology at Furman University on July 30, 1856, remains a monument and a map for training ministers.[25] Its application to the churches of the Lord Jesus would be a wise step as well. He hoped to "see the means of theological education increased … open to all who would embrace them."[26] Would it not be wonderful to see this vision become a reality in our local fellowships?

Addressing a commitment to sound biblical doctrine, Boyce issued both a warning and a challenge: "It is with a single man that error usually commences; and when such a man has influence or position, it is impossible to estimate the evil that will attend it. Ecclesiastical history is full of warning upon this subject. Scarcely a single heresy has ever blighted the Church which has not owed its existence or its development to that one man of power and ability whose name has always been associated with its doctrines."[27] Given this ever-present danger, churches should expect their teachers to teach in accordance with and not contrary to their doctrinal statements. To do so is right, honest, and fair.

Southern Baptists must produce and foster a positive theological agenda, not merely one that is defensive and reactionary. We must teach biblical doctrine, love biblical doctrine, and proclaim biblical doctrine. The place where this can most effectively be accomplished is in the local church. Baptists have a long history of providing organized instruction in biblical doctrine. Most churches have a Sunday School organization for Bible teaching and a discipleship organization that teaches members sound biblical doctrine and principles for applying biblical truth to life.

We must teach biblical doctrine, love biblical doctrine, and proclaim biblical doctrine.

Match each of the following statements with the church distinctive to which it most closely relates.

___ 1. Methods can be created and adapted to share the timeless truths of the gospel in a changing society.

___ 2. "Brothers, if someone is caught in any wrongdoing, you who are spiritual should restore such a person with a gentle spirit, watching out for yourselves so you won't be tempted also" (Gal. 6:1).

___ 3. The Lord's Supper and baptism are ordinances that Christians do as acts of obedience, symbolism, and remembrance.

___ 4. Each congregation operates under the lordship of Christ through democratic processes.

___ 5. We must teach biblical doctrine, love biblical doctrine, and proclaim biblical doctrine.

___ 6. "… a famine through the land: not a famine of bread or a thirst for water, but of hearing the words of the Lord" (Amos 8:11).

___ 7. The membership of a local church is made up of those who repent of sin and confess Christ as Savior and Lord.

a. Regenerate church membership

b. The ordinances

c. Church discipline

d. A Word-based ministry

e. A biblical ecclesiology of leadership and governance

f. Missions and evangelism

g. Sound theology

Answers: 1. f, 2. c, 3. b, 4. e, 5. g, 6. d, 7. a

Seven marks or distinctives of a New Testament church are listed below. Prayerfully evaluate your church in reflecting each distinctive. Place an *X* in the appropriate place on each scale.

Regenerate church membership:

Improvement needed   Good   Outstanding

Ordinances:

Improvement needed   Good   Outstanding

Church discipline:

Improvement needed   Good   Outstanding

Word-based ministry:

Improvement needed   Good   Outstanding

Biblical ecclesiology of leadership and governance:

Improvement needed   Good   Outstanding

Missions and evangelism:

Improvement needed   Good   Outstanding

Sound theology:

Improvement needed   Good   Outstanding

A SOBERING REFLECTION

Mark was unusually quiet after his efforts to help Jim understand the characteristics of a true New Testament church. Finally, Mark spoke: "It's been a long time since I've thought about what distinguishes a church from other organizations. I don't think most churchgoers think about the church as a dynamic, living organization that changes and grows and struggles with who it is, who it should be, and who it is becoming. If we thought more about these marks of the church, our debates might be more informed. Maybe people like you wouldn't drop out and stay out."

Mark continued, "Jim, the reason you don't see most of our churches as any different from other organizations is that they aren't. At least on the surface they don't appear much different to the average member. In my own church fewer than half of the members attend on a given Sunday. We are no different from the typical Southern Baptist church. But now I think I know why."

Mark paused for a while, allowing Jim to ask why.

"This study has convicted me. I honestly think our church doesn't have a clue whether people who present themselves for membership are truly Christians. We do little more than ask them to come forward and fill out a membership card. We should be more proactive in making sure people understand what it means to be a Christian and a member of the body of Christ."

The two men were beginning to see the importance of the church. But they were also learning that most of the churches in their community didn't look like a true New Testament church. It's little wonder that the back doors of these churches are open wide.

But this study only whetted their appetites for more. They agreed to spend the next week trying to get a better grasp on how churches are supposed to be organized and make decisions. We will hear from them again in the next chapter.

🔍 Review your memory verses for this chapter.

🔍 Spend time in prayer thanking God for your church and asking Him to help your church faithfully reflect the marks of a New Testament church.

LEADER GUIDE

Session 2

IS MY CHURCH ACTING LIKE THE CHURCH?

BEFORE THE SESSION

1. Study chapter 2 and complete the learning activities.
2. Write the following Scripture references and instructions on separate index cards: Group 1: *John 17:20-21; Acts 4:32; Galatians 3:27-28; Ephesians 4:4-6.* Group 2: *Ephesians 5:25-27; 1 Thessalonians 4:3; 1 Peter 1:14-16.* Group 3: *Ephesians 1:22-23; Colossians 1:17-18; Hebrews 12:22-23.* Group 4: *Ephesians 2:19-20; Jude 3.*

DURING THE SESSION

1. State the topic of chapter 2. Ask a volunteer to lead in prayer.
2. Write on a dry-erase board: *Christians believe in one holy, catholic and apostolic church.* Underline the words *one, holy, catholic,* and *apostolic.* Explain that this description of the church comes from the Council of Constantinople that met in A.D. 381. Explain that *catholic* means *universal.* Divide members into four groups and give each group a card with Scripture references. Ask each group to read its Scriptures and to decide which mark of the church is revealed. Allow time for work and call for reports. Answers: group 1, *one;* group 2, *holy;* group 3, *universal;* group 4, *apostolic.*
3. Direct attention to the true/false activity on page 39. Lead the group to respond to and discuss the statements.
4. Write these Latin terms on a dry-erase board: *sola Scriptura, sola gratia, sola fide.* Lead the group to define them. Ask: *Why is Scripture alone the source of Christian revelation? Why is the statement* Scripture alone *important? Do all Christians hold to this statement? What are other sources of Christian revelation for some people? Why is salvation God's free gift? How is salvation made possible? What part does human merit play in salvation? What is faith? Can a person be saved apart from faith?*
5. State: *We can discover the characteristics of a New Testament church by studying the early churches. Seven essential characteristics are evident.* Write on a dry-erase board: *1. Regenerate Church Membership.* Ask: *What is a believers' church? Why does our church insist that only believers can belong? What are evidences that the early churches consisted of believers only? What can happen if a church admits nonbelievers as members? What*

are the different ways our church receives persons for membership? What can our church do to make sure that only true believers are admitted to membership?

6. Write on a dry-erase board: *2. The Ordinances.* Ask: *What is an ordinance? What is a sacrament? What is the difference between an ordinance and a sacrament? How many church ordinances does a church observe?*

7. Direct attention to the agree/disagree activity on page 44. Lead the group to respond to and discuss the statements.

8. Direct attention to the agree/disagree activity on page 45. Lead the group to respond to and discuss the statements. Ask: *What is most meaningful to you about observing the Lord's Supper? How can we make this ordinance more meaningful to our members?*

9. Write on a dry-erase board: *3. Church Discipline.* Point out that session 4 will be devoted to this mark of a New Testament church.

10. Write on a dry-erase board: *4. A Word-Based Ministry.* Ask: *What is a Word-based ministry? What is meant by the inerrancy of Scripture? What is meant by the sufficiency of Scripture? How does* sola *Scriptura relate to a Word-based ministry? What are some evidences that our church practices a Word-based ministry?*

11. Write on a dry-erase board: *5. A Biblical Ecclesiology of Leadership and Governance.* Point out that session 3 will be devoted to polity, or church governance.

12. Write on a dry-erase board: *6. Missions and Evangelism.* Ask: *What is meant by the statement "Evangelism and missions are in our Southern Baptist DNA"? What is the teaching of inclusivism? How is inclusivism seen in our world today? What is the difference between evangelism and missions? What are some ways our church is involved in evangelism? What are some ways our church is involved in missions?*

13. Write on a dry-erase board: *7. Sound Theology.* Ask: *Why does a church need to be vigilant about sound biblical doctrine? What can happen if false doctrine is taught in the church? What are some ways our church teaches Bible doctrine? How can Sunday School be strengthened in our church? How can discipleship training be strengthened in our church?*

14. Direct attention to the matching activity on page 53. Ask volunteers to read the seven statements and to match them with the seven marks you have recorded on the dry-erase board.

15. As a group, evaluate your church in regard to the seven marks, using the scale on page 54.

16. Call on volunteers to recite the memory verse from chapter 1. As a group, read aloud the memory verses for chapter 2. Encourage the group to continue memorizing Scripture. Close with prayer, asking God to help your church always reflect the characteristics of a New Testament church.

17. Ask members to read chapter 3 and to complete the activities before the next session.

Chapter 3

HOW DOES A VIBRANT CHURCH MAKE DECISIONS?

Learning Goals

A study of this chapter will help you gain a better understanding of church government. You will learn the qualifications and responsibilities of the pastor(s) and deacons, and you will be motivated to pray for them daily.

Memory Verses

"He personally gave some to be apostles, some prophets, some evangelists, some pastors and teachers, for the training of the saints in the work of ministry, to build up the body of Christ, until we all reach unity in the faith and in the knowledge of God's Son, growing into a mature man with a stature measured by Christ's fullness" (Eph. 4:11-13).

"Sometimes I wonder," Mark confessed to Jim, "if my church is really a New Testament church at all."

Jim was surprised at his friend's forthright statement. "Now wait a minute, Mark," Jim responded. "I'm the one who is supposed to have all the questions about the church. After all, I have been out of church for several years, and you have attended faithfully."

"I know," Mark said, "but this study of the church has really opened my eyes. I am surprised to see how far we seem to have drifted from the biblical model of a church."

"Well, we are about to study the organization of the church," Jim said. "How does your church function? How does it make decisions?"

"Let's see," Mark began. "We've had three pastors in eight years. Some people thought one was a dictator. We have a committee system, but sometimes it doesn't seem very efficient. And we have monthly business meetings, but sometimes the decisions we make seem trivial to me. There must be a better way."

CHURCH ORGANIZATION

The way a Baptist church makes decisions is often a sight to behold. Think about it: a nervous pastor, monthly business meetings dedicated to unimportant issues, a committee structure that looks like the bureaucracies of some governmental agencies, and a deacon body that functions like a corporate-business board. This is not what the Bible teaches about church government.

In broad terms there are five forms of church government or polity:

1. *Episcopal—Roman Catholics, Anglicans/Episcopalians, Methodists.* Churches with episcopal polity are governed in groups called dioceses with hierarchical leadership. These levels of leadership have various names, depending on the faith tradition. Some traditions also have lay councils within the church. Each diocese is led by a bishop, who supervises pastors.

2. *Presbyterian.* Most typified by the Presbyterian church, this type of church government is executed by a system of councils. The lowest level is the local church, whose council is called a session. Other levels include the presbytery and synods, or general assemblies. Members of the session are called elders, who are elected by the congregation. The pastor is sometimes called the teaching elder.

Polity: church government

Congregation-alism: a form of church government holding that the authority of the church resides in each local body of believers

Forms of church government:
- **Episcopal**
- **Presbyterian**
- **Congregational**
- **Erastian**
- **Minimalist or nongovernmental**

3. *Congregational—Baptists, Congregationalists, some Lutherans.* In churches that practice congregational polity, the congregation is the ultimate decision-making group. The pastor may be the leader or the presiding officer, but he does not have final say in making decisions; the congregation does. Local churches are autonomous, meaning they govern themselves, though they may choose to affiliate with other churches, usually within the same denominational group, on various levels—local, state, and/or national. These associations do not govern the churches; however, a church can be excluded if the church holds theology, doctrine, or practice that differs from the mainstream beliefs of that denomination.

4. *Erastian.* National state churches are governed by a secular leader. Citizens are members by virtue of their birth in that country unless they opt to become members of a nonstate church. Taxes support the church. Some Scandinavians have Christian state churches; for example, the Lutheran church is the state church of Norway.

5. *Minimalist or nongovernmental—Quakers, Plymouth Brethren.* This style of church governance is simple, with as little administration as possible. Emphasis is on the individual's experience rather than the group experience. Members of the congregation make decisions by seeking unity, with every member being equal.[1]

Match the following descriptions with the correct forms of church government.

_____ 1. Virtually all governmental structure is eliminated.

_____ 2. Local churches govern themselves, with no external power over them.

_____ 3. Levels of leadership make up a hierarchical system, with bishops who supervise pastors.

_____ 4. National state churches are governed by a secular leader.

_____ 5. This is a representative system of councils using elders elected by the congregation.

a. Episcopal

b. Presbyterian

c. Congregational

d. Erastian

e. Minimalist or nongovernmental

Beneath each form of church government in the previous activity, write the name of one denomination or group that practices that form. Check your work in the foregoing paragraphs.

Each of these systems has positive, even commendable features; and each seeks to highlight particular features of church government found in Scripture. However, an examination of God's Word reveals that New Testament churches were basically congregational. The exact nature of this congregationalism may have varied; but at its most basic level, churches were local bodies of baptized believers who operated within the parameters of congregationalism. We will begin by examining the evidence for congregational organization or polity in the local church.

"Not many should become teachers, my brothers, knowing that we will receive a stricter judgment."
James 3:1

THE NEW TESTAMENT MODEL OF CHURCH GOVERNMENT

Congregationalism affirms that the authority of the church resides in each local body of believers. No person or organization is above it except Jesus Christ. He alone is its head. Each member has equal rights and responsibilities. However, aspects of representative democracy are not ruled out. The body of believers may select certain persons to lead and serve in specific ways. Leaders in a local congregation are ultimately answerable to God (see Heb. 13:17; Jas. 3:1; 1 Pet. 5:2-4), but they are also responsible to the congregation.

"Shepherd God's flock among you, not overseeing out of compulsion but freely, according to God's will; not for the money but eagerly; not lording it over those entrusted to you, but being examples to the flock. And when the chief Shepherd appears, you will receive the unfading crown of glory."
1 Peter 5:2-4

Mark each statement *T* (true) or *F* (false) as it relates to the congregational form of church polity.
____ 1. The pastor has authority over the church.
____ 2. The local congregation is independent and self-governing.
____ 3. The local congregation is the seat of authority.
____ 4. Decisions made by the local congregation can be overruled by the local Baptist association.
____ 5. No person or organization is above the local congregation except Jesus Christ.
____ 6. The pastor is accountable to both God and the congregation.

Several key Scripture passages provide the foundation for our understanding of congregational church government.

True: 2, 3, 5, 6

False: 1, 4

Matthew 18:15-17. This is one of two texts (the other is Matt. 16:18) in the Gospels that use the word *church (ekklesia)*. The issue in this text was how the believing community was to deal with a sinning brother or sister. The text follows a pattern rooted in Deuteronomy 17:6; 19:15 and is consistent with other practices of the day.[2]

Read Matthew 18:15-17 in the margin. Complete the sentence.

In matters of church discipline, the final authority is _____.

The text indicates that the final court of appeal in the exercise of church discipline is the church and "that each member of the church is to abide by the corporate judgment."[3] Mark Dever points out, "Notice to whom one finally appeals in such situations. What court has the final word? It is not a bishop, a pope, or a presbytery; it is not an assembly, a synod, a convention, or a conference. It is not even a pastor or a board of elders, a board of deacons or a church committee. It is, quite simply, the church— that is, the assembly of those individual believers who are the church."[4]

Acts 6:1-7. The church was confronted with a problem about ministry—how daily distributions for widows should take place and who would be responsible for the task. The fact that the apostles were involved in the way the decision was reached makes what we find all the more remarkable. Verses 2-3 say that the twelve summoned the multitude of disciples and urged them to "select from among you seven men of good reputation … whom we can appoint to this duty."

Read Acts 6:1-7. Complete the following sentence.

The seven helpers were selected by _____.

Verse 5 reveals that "the proposal pleased the whole company. So they chose Stephen." They (the whole multitude) then brought these men before the apostles, who "prayed and laid hands on them" (v. 6). Notice the congregational involvement, initiated by the apostles, in seeking men who would serve. This strategy balances congregational participation with pastoral leadership. This passage shows the wisdom of strong pastoral leadership and appropriate congregational involvement.

"If your brother sins against you, go and rebuke him in private. If he listens to you, you have won your brother. But if he won't listen, take one or two more with you, so that 'by the testimony of two or three witnesses every fact may be established.' If he pays no attention to them, tell the church. But if he doesn't pay attention even to the church, let him be like an unbeliever and a tax collector to you."

Matthew 18:15-17

Acts 11:22. The church in Antioch was the first and most prominent missionary fellowship in the early days of the church. When the gospel came to Antioch, those in Jerusalem wanted to help and encourage the work there.

Read Acts 11:19-24. Complete the following sentence.

Barnabas was sent to Antioch by _____ .

Verse 22 informs us that the church in Jerusalem "sent out Barnabas to travel as far as Antioch." He was not sent by the apostles or the elders only. The clear indication is that the congregation as a whole sent him.

Acts 14:27. Paul and Barnabas returned to Antioch following the first missionary journey (see Acts 13:1–14:28).

Read Acts 14:26-28. Complete the following sentence.

At the end of their first missionary journey, Paul and Barnabas reported to _____ .

"After they arrived and gathered the church together, they reported everything God had done with them" (v. 27). Their report was not to the leadership only but to the entire congregation.

Acts 15. This passage records the crucial meeting of the Jerusalem conference to determine the status of Gentiles in the church and to settle issues related to salvation and the keeping of the law.

Read Acts 15:1-35. Complete the following sentences.

The men to accompany Paul and Barnabas to Antioch with the letter were selected by the apostles, the elders, and _____ .
The letter was delivered to _____ .

This text is crucial in shedding light on issues of local-church autonomy, voluntary cooperation among churches, and church polity.
1. The local church in Antioch sent Paul and Barnabas to Jerusalem (see 15:2-3), and the local church in Jerusalem received them, along with the apostles and elders (see 15:4).

"From there they sailed back to Antioch where they had been entrusted to the grace of God for the work they had completed. After they arrived and gathered the church together, they reported everything God had done with them, and that He had opened the door of faith to the Gentiles. And they spent a considerable time with the disciples."

Acts 14:26-28

2. The decision by the church in Antioch to send Paul and Barnabas to Jerusalem to confer with the apostles and elders about the Gentile question arose from that church's voluntary initiative.

3. Though the apostles and elders appropriately convened and led the discussion, "the whole assembly ... listened" (15:12).

4. Verse 22 points out that "the apostles and the elders, with the whole church, decided to select men from among them" to deliver, along with Paul and Barnabas, the decision reached by the conference in Jerusalem.

5. The letter that was sent came from "the apostles and the elders, your brothers,"[5] and it was directed to "the brothers" (the church as a whole) in Antioch (see 15:23).

6. The church as a whole received the letter (see 15:30) and rejoiced over its content (see 15:31). In all that took place, congregational involvement and action were present at every turn.

In all that took place, congregational involvement and action were present at every turn.

1 Corinthians 5. The issue was church discipline (see Matt 18:15-17). Sexual immorality had gone unchecked, and Paul was scandalized by the church's lax behavior and indifferent attitude. Paul addressed the congregation as a whole. In particular, he stated that appropriate discipline is to be exercised "when you are assembled" (v. 4). Church discipline is a matter to be handled by the entire congregation, not just by those in leadership. Paul called for a "community action, carried out in the context of the Spirit. ... The whole community must carry out the action."[6]

1 Corinthians 6. The issue here was Christians suing Christians in civil courts. Again outraged by such an action, Paul rebuked the Corinthians. To whom should believers appeal when situations of this nature arise? Paul provided the answer in verse 1: the saints. He did not say a presbytery, an assembly, a synod, a board of elders, a pastor, a group of deacons, or a church committee. This issue is the responsibility of the entire body. Although the church may choose to delegate the responsibility to gifted, qualified persons to handle such matters (doing so is not inconsistent with congregationalism), ultimately, the adjudication of the issue rests with the local congregation as a whole.

1 Corinthians 16. Taking a collection for the church in Jerusalem, Paul told the congregation, as a body of believers, what they should do. Further, to ensure proper accountability and integrity, the church was to approve those who would go to Jerusalem with its gift (see 16:3-4).

2 Corinthians 2. The issue once more was church discipline. Paul says that in the matter of church discipline, "the punishment by the majority is sufficient for such a person." Kruse says the text "suggests that the congregation had acted formally and judicially against the offender."[7] It seems clear that a church vote took place and that the congregation as a local body of believers took part in the process. Congregational polity undergirds another distinctive mark of a vibrant church: the practice of church discipline, which will be addressed in chapter 4.[8]

THEOLOGICAL EVIDENCE FOR CONGREGATIONALISM

When we reflect theologically on what the Bible teaches about church government and polity, the case for congregationalism only gets stronger.

Responsibility for doctrine and practice. Saucy notes, "The responsibility of maintaining true doctrine and practice is directed toward the entire church."[9] While the leaders of the church are especially responsible and accountable in this area (see Acts 20:28-32; 1 Thess. 5:12-13; 1 Tim. 3:2; 2 Tim. 2:1-2; 4:1-5; Titus 1:9; Jas. 3:1; 1 Pet. 5:2), the calling to pursue doctrinal fidelity "is ultimately held in trust, under God, by the congregation."[10] Consider these examples.

- First Corinthians 11:17-34 rebukes the church in Corinth as a whole for disgracing the Lord's Supper.
- Galatians 1:8-9 places the burden for maintaining the purity of the gospel in the hands of local churches.
- First Thessalonians 5:21 admonishes each believer to "test all things. Hold on to what is good."
- First John 2:20,27 speaks of the Spirit's anointing and every believer's ability to understand the truth.
- First John 4:1 challenges each believer to "test the spirits to determine if they are from God."
- Jude, written "to those who are the called, loved by God the Father, and kept by Jesus Christ" (Jude 1), calls on each one of us "to contend for the faith that was delivered to the saints once for all" (Jude 3). The faith was delivered to all believers.

It is crucial to see that whenever Scripture combats false teaching, it addresses the churches because doctrinal integrity is a matter of congregational responsibility.

Theological evidence for congregationalism:
- **Responsibility for doctrine and practice**
- **Cessation of the apostolic office**
- **Church order and unity**
- **The priesthood of believers**
- **Scripture alone**

Cessation of the apostolic office. The apostles had a special, unique position of authority and leadership in the first-century churches. However, even the apostles, as we have seen, did not exercise absolute and unlimited authority. D. A. Carson analyzes the situation well:

> Arguably, the strongest authoritative human voices in the earliest churches were the apostles (in the narrow sense of that flexible term, i.e., the Twelve [Matthias replacing Judas] plus Paul). Their authority extended beyond the local congregation, even beyond congregations they had been instrumental in founding (for how else could Peter's influence be felt in Corinth and Paul's in Colossae?), but it was not without limit. A Peter could prove inconsistent in practice (Gal 2:11-14) and a Paul could be mistaken in judgment (Acts 15:37-40; cf. 2 Tim 4:11). The objective truth of the gospel, Paul insists, enjoys an antecedent authority; if even an apostle tampers with that, he is to be reckoned anathema (Gal 1:8-9).[11]

It is significant to note that there is no mention of the transference of the apostolic office. Once the apostles were dead, the office died with them. The absence of successors to the apostles is due to the uniqueness of their office. Directly commissioned by Christ Himself (see Mark 3:14), the disciples were sent forth as His representatives with His authority (see Matt. 10:40). Only Christ's apostles met the necessary qualifications. They must bear direct witness to the resurrection (see Acts 1:21-22) and receive their commission and teaching ultimately from Him (see 1 Cor. 9:1; Gal. 1:1,11-17). These roles could not be passed on. After the apostles died, the responsibility for carrying out the work of the church transitioned to the congregation.

Church order and unity. Because the church is a body, an interrelatedness connects each member to one another. Together all members share the load of congregational responsibility. The church in Corinth struggled with proper decorum in worship. Paul did not instruct just the leadership but the entire congregation to "let all things be done decently and in order" (1 Cor. 14:39-40). The church in Philippi had two women who had a personal conflict of some sort. The responsibility to help them work things out was given to the local body as a whole (see Phil. 4:1-3).

Together all members share the load of congregational responsibility.

The priesthood of believers. The priesthood of believers is the belief that every Christian has direct access to God through Christ without a human mediator and that every Christian is to serve as a priest on behalf of others. Theologically, this biblical concept is important evidence for congregational polity. Two other Baptist distinctives, soul competency and religious liberty, though closely related to priesthood of the believer, must not be equated with this doctrine.

Soul competency, the conviction that all people have an inalienable right of direct access to God, applies to all people without discrimination. Soul competency is a natural component of being created in God's image. However, the effects of the fall have greatly injured humankind's ability to relate to God. Indeed, without His initiation, we will not seek Him, and we will suppress and pervert His revelation (see Rom. 1:18–3:20). Soul competency affirms that every individual is responsible to God, and it motivates us to share the gospel with everyone. Timothy George summarizes the doctrine well and then relates it to the doctrine of the priesthood of believers: "Soul competency pertains universally to all persons, not merely to Christians. Baptists, however, do not teach the 'priesthood of all human beings.' Priesthood applies only to those who, through repentance and faith, have been admitted into the covenant of grace and, consequently, have been made participants in the priestly ministry of their Mediator, Jesus Christ, i.e., to believers only."[12]

Priesthood of believers: the belief that every Christian has direct access to God through Christ without a human mediator and that every Christian is to serve as a priest on behalf of others

Soul competency: the belief that all people have an inalienable right of direct access to God

Mark each statement *T* (true) or *F* (false).

_____ 1. Soul competency pertains to all persons, not just Christians.

_____ 2. The priesthood of believers emphasizes both freedom and responsibility.

_____ 3. The doctrine of the priesthood of believers emphasizes the individual, not the community.

_____ 4. Soul competency relates to human achievement and accomplishment.

_____ 5. The priesthood of believers has implications for a believer's service.

_____ 6. Soul competency affirms that every individual is responsible to God.

_____ 7. Soul competency is a natural component of being created in God's image.

_____ 8. Every Christian is to serve as a priest on behalf of others.

True: 1, 2, 5, 6, 7, 8

False: 3, 4

Religious liberty: a congregation's right to order its own internal life, doctrine, and discipline, in accordance with its understanding of divine truth

Religious liberty guarantees every congregation the right to order its own internal life, doctrine, and discipline, in accordance with its understanding of divine truth. No external entity may intrude or interfere with the internal governance and workings of this voluntary association. George is correct in what this entails: "Practically, this means that heresy is always possible and that spiritual vigilance is a constant necessity. Thus, priesthood of believers does not mean, 'I am a priest. I can believe anything I want to.' It means rather, 'As a priest in a covenanted community of believers, I must be alert to keep my congregation from departing from "the faith once and for all delivered unto the saints" ' (Jude 3)."[13] It is clear, therefore, that soul competency, religious liberty, and the priesthood of believers are interrelated but not identical theological tenets.

The priesthood of believers was a major emphasis of the Reformation in the 16th century. It was recovered by the reformers to strengthen "an evangelical understanding of the church. … In modern theology, however, the ecclesial context of this Reformation principle has been almost totally eclipsed." The reformers made a crucial distinction that is often missed. They did not speak of the priesthood of the believer. "The reformers talked instead of the 'priesthood of all believers' (plural). For them it was never a question of a lonely, isolated seeker of truth, but rather of a band of faithful believers united in a common confession."[14]

The priesthood of believers does not mean, "I am my own priest." It means that in the community of saints, we are all priests to one another. The priesthood of believers has to do with the believer's service. This truth does not negate individual gifts or calling. Rather, it enhances our giftedness as we individually and collectively do our part to build the body (see Eph. 4:11-16). The priesthood of believers is a crucial scriptural teaching that is totally consistent with congregationalism.

Scripture alone. The Bible as the Word of God is a believer's sole authority for faith and practice. It teaches what to believe and how to live. The responsibility to live under the lordship of Jesus Christ is directly related to every believer's obedience to the Word. The work of the Spirit, in concert with the Word, equips and qualifies a believer to judge and test all things. This responsibility is not limited to a special group within the church, not even the leadership. Doctrinal accountability is the responsibility of all believers in the body of Christ as they submit themselves to the lordship of Christ under the authority of His Word.

The New Testament thus reveals a consistent, overarching pattern of congregational church government and polity. In addition, it provides theological support for congregational church government.

Read each Scripture reference and match it with the statement to which it best refers.

____ 1. 1 John 4:1	a. Christ has made all believers priests.
____ 2. Mark 3:14	b. The apostles were directly commissioned by Christ.
____ 3. 1 Corinthians 14:39-40	c. All believers are responsible for guarding against false teachings.
____ 4. Revelation 1:5-6; 5:9-10	d. The entire congregation is responsible for order and unity.

Answers: 1. c, 2. b, 3. d, 4. a

SPIRITUAL LEADERSHIP IN A NEW TESTAMENT CHURCH

Read Philippians 1:1 and complete the following sentence.

Paul wrote to all the saints in Philippi, including the _____

and the _____ .

New Testament churches also serve as our model for the spiritual leaders of a vibrant church. In the New Testament church there were only two offices within each congregation—pastors and deacons (see Phil. 1:1; 1 Tim. 3:1-13). The pastor was the spiritual leader of the church, just as pastors are the spiritual leaders of Southern Baptist churches today. The pastor is the first among equals, the leader of a congregational, democratic form of church government and leadership. Therefore, he does not necessarily practice an authoritarian leadership style, though this style is more evident in some independent churches.

In recent years a small number of Baptist churches have moved away from congregational polity and adopted rule by a board of elders, as in a classic presbyterian type of governance and leadership. LifeWay Research indicates that fewer than 5 percent of Baptist churches follow this form of

"Paul and Timothy, slaves of Christ Jesus: To all the saints in Christ Jesus who are in Philippi, including the overseers and deacons."

Philippians 1:1

polity. We are not advocating this trend, just reporting it. We will look at New Testament teachings and address the subject of elders from a leadership perspective.

In New Testament churches God raised up and qualified, by the work of the Holy Spirit, men who were appointed to exercise oversight and spiritual care for the churches. The New Testament calls these men elders, bishops, or pastors. In Scripture the three terms are interchangeable, and all are used for the same office. According to *The Baptist Faith and Message*, the Greek word translated *pastor* is interchangeable with the words *elder* and *bishop*. The New Testament also uses the terms *elder* and *overseer* interchangeably.[15] This view was defined by numerous church fathers, including Jerome, who stated, "Indeed with the ancients these names were synonymous, one alluding to the office, the other to the age of the clergy."[16]

The Greek term *presbuteros (elder)* and its cognates appear 66 times in the New Testament. This word can refer to an old person (man or woman; see John 8:9; Acts 2:17; 1 Tim. 5:1-2). More commonly, the word denotes officials in both Judaism (members of the Sanhedrin or synagogue) and the church. In a few places it has the meaning of *forefathers* (see Matt. 15:2; Mark 7:3,5; Heb. 11:2). We find various designations associated with elders: elders of the people (see Matt. 21:23; 26:3, 47; 27:1; Luke 22:66), elders of the Jews (see Luke 7:3; Acts 15:15), elders of Israel (see Acts 4:8), and elders of the church (see Acts 20:17; Jas. 5:14). There were elders in the churches of Jerusalem (see Acts 11:30; 15:2,4,6,22-23; 16:4; 21:18), Galatia (see Acts 14:23), Ephesus (see Acts 20:17; 1 Tim. 5:17,19), Crete (see Titus 1:5), Asia Minor (see 1 Pet. 5:1), and other Jewish Christian assemblies (see Jas. 5:14).

The first time *elders* is used in a specifically Christian context is in Acts 11:30, in which the church in Antioch sent Barnabas and Paul to the elders in Jerusalem with money to aid in famine relief (see 11:27-30). It is interesting that the term appears without any explanation. In Acts 14:23 Paul and Barnabas "appointed elders in every church," and in Acts 20:17 Paul's farewell speech is given to the elders of Ephesus. Other references to elders occur in 1 Timothy 5:17,19: Titus 1:5; Hebrews 11:2 *(forefathers);* James 5:14; 1 Peter 5:1; 5:2; 2 John 1; 3 John 1; and 12 occurrences in the Book of Revelation.

Scriptural leadership in a New Testament church:
- **Pastors**
- **Deacons**

Presbuteros

(Greek): **elder**

Read Acts 20:17-31 and complete the following sentences.

Paul sent to Ephesus for the _____ of the church (v. 17).

Paul said the Holy Spirit had appointed the elders as _____ (v. 28).

Paul said their job was to _____ the church of God (v. 28).

Answers: elders, overseers, shepherd

The word *episkopos* (*overseer,* also translated *bishop)* occurs five times in the New Testament. In Acts 20:28 Paul told the Ephesian elders that the Holy Spirit had made them overseers and that they were to shepherd the church of God. Here all three crucial terms with respect to church leadership appear. Elders oversee and shepherd the flock. Notice that the two terms (*elder* and *overseer)* are used interchangeably. In his salutation to the church in Philippi, Paul addressed all the saints, including the overseers and deacons (see Phil. 1:1). First Timothy 3:2-7 and Titus 1:7-9 list the qualifications for overseers. First Peter 2:25 refers to Christ as "the Shepherd and Overseer of your souls."

The word *poimen,* which occurs numerous times in the New Testament, can be translated *pastor* or *shepherd.* The term *poimen* is used of those "called by God to feed, care for, and lead His people, who are His flock."[17] Ephesians 4:11 refers to those gifted as pastors. First Peter 5:1-2 address elders who are to shepherd God's flock, giving oversight (NASB, HCSB) or serving as overseers (NIV). Again, all three terms converge and are used interchangeably in this passage.

Episkopos
(Greek): **overseer or bishop**

Poimen *(Greek):* **pastor or shepherd**

Match each descriptive statement with the correct term.

___ 1. Refers to the wisdom and maturity of the pastor as he guides the church

___ 2. Refers to the pastor's administrative role in leading the church

___ 3. Refers to the pastor's role as shepherd to care for and feed God's people

a. Pastor
b. Bishop or overseer
c. Elder

"Be on guard for yourselves and for all the flock, among whom the Holy Spirit has appointed you as overseers, to shepherd the church of God, which He purchased with His own blood."

Acts 20:28

Answers: 1. c, 2. b, 3. a

Describe one way your pastor cares for and feeds
your congregation.

_____

_____

_____

_____

Describe one way your pastor's administrative role is reflected
as he leads your church.

_____

_____

_____

_____

Describe one way your pastor's wisdom and maturity
are reflected as he guides your church.

_____

_____

_____

_____

QUALIFICATIONS AND RESPONSIBILITIES[18]

The most important issue for church leadership is spiritual integrity. Any man who would serve in this capacity must be biblically qualified. Nothing is more important. No office of the church is to be held by spiritually unqualified or disqualified men. Scripture makes it clear that God is most concerned with the character and service of those who lead His church. Four texts in particular stand out with respect to God's expectations for those who would shepherd, lead, or oversee His churches: Acts 20:17-38; 1 Timothy 3:1-7; Titus 1:5-9; and 1 Peter 5:1-4. Additional texts that address expectations for spiritual leaders and the congregations that follow them include 1 Corinthians 16:15-16; Galatians 6:6; Ephesians 4:11-16; 1 Thessalonians 5:12-13; 1 Timothy 5:17-25; and Hebrews 13:7,17,24.

Read 1 Timothy 3:1-7. List the qualifications for a pastor as revealed in this passage.

_____

_____

_____

_____

_____

_____

_____

_____

_____

_____

_____

> " 'If anyone aspires to be an overseer, he desires a noble work.' An overseer, therefore, must be above reproach, the husband of one wife, self-controlled, sensible, respectable, hospitable, an able teacher, not addicted to wine, not a bully but gentle, not quarrelsome, not greedy—one who manages his own household competently, having his children under control with all dignity. (If anyone does not know how to manage his own household, how will he take care of God's church?) He must not be a new convert, or he might become conceited and fall into the condemnation of the Devil. Furthermore, he must have a good reputation among outsiders, so that he does not fall into disgrace and the Devil's trap."
>
> 1 Timothy 3:1-7

Read Titus 1:5-9. Add any additional qualifications given in this passage.

Read 1 Peter 5:1-4. Add any additional qualifications found in this passage.

> "The reason I left you in Crete was to set right what was left undone and, as I directed you, to appoint elders in every town: someone who is blameless, the husband of one wife, having faithful children not accused of wildness or rebellion. For an overseer, as God's manager, must be blameless, not arrogant, not quick tempered, not addicted to wine, not a bully, not greedy for money, but hospitable, loving what is good, sensible, righteous, holy, self-controlled, holding to the faithful message as taught, so that he will be able both to encourage with sound teaching and to refute those who contradict it."
>
> **Titus 1:5-9**

Anyone serving as an elder, an overseer, or a pastor is expected to meet *all* of the qualifications for the office—including a call to ministry and an ability to teach. What are the responsibilities and qualifications, as outlined in Scripture?

Responsibilities of a pastor/elder/overseer:
- Overall responsibility for the oversight and direction of the church (see 1 Thess. 5:12; Heb. 13:17)
- Responsible to seek in all matters the mind of Christ (the head of the church) through the guidance of the Holy Spirit and the Word of God (see Eph. 1:22; Col. 1:18; 1 Pet. 5:2)
- Able to teach, able to exhort the church in sound doctrine and ready to refute those who contradict the truth (see Eph. 4:11-12; 1 Tim. 3:2; Titus 1:9)
- Provides instruction for the maintenance of healthy relationships in the church (see Gal. 6:1; 1 Thess. 5:12; 2 Thess. 3:14-15)

- Exercises at least general oversight of the financial matters of the church (see Acts 11:30)
- Leads (with appropriate congregational input) in appointing deacons as necessary to accomplish the mission of the church (see Acts 6:1-6)
- Leads by example (see Heb. 13:7; 1 Pet. 5:2-3)
- Leads in the exercise of church discipline (see Gal. 6:1) but not to the exclusion of the entire body when warranted (see Matt. 18:15-17; 1 Cor. 5; 2 Cor. 2:5-12)

Read Ephesians 4:11-13. State two responsibilities of pastors (v. 12).

1. _____

2. _____

State the overall goal of their work (v. 13).

_____

_____

"He personally gave some to be apostles, some prophets, some evangelists, some pastors and teachers, for the training of the saints in the work of ministry, to build up the body of Christ, until we all reach unity in the faith and in the knowledge of God's Son, growing into a mature man with a stature measured by Christ's fullness."

Ephesians 4:11-13

Qualifications of a pastor/elder/overseer:

- Must be above reproach—blameless, having unimpeachable integrity, no grounds for accusation of improper Christian behavior (see 1 Tim. 3:2; Titus 1:6)
- Husband of one wife. He has only one woman in his life, and he is faithful to her (see 1 Tim. 3:2; Titus 1:6).
- Demonstrates self-control. He is not in bondage to himself or the desires of the flesh. He is temperate, calm, sober, and collected in spirit (see 1 Tim. 3:2; Titus 1:8).
- Sensible, prudent, wise, balanced in judgment. He is not given to quick, superficial decisions based on immature thinking (see 1 Tim. 3:2; Titus 1:8).
- Respectable, demonstrating good behavior and an orderly life (see 1 Tim. 3:2)
- Hospitable, generous, a lover of strangers, and willing to share with others (see 1 Tim. 3:2; Titus 1:8)

- Able to teach. He can communicate the truth of God to others and exhort them in sound doctrine (see 1 Tim. 3:2; Titus 1:9).
- Not addicted to wine. He is not a drunkard, not controlled by but free from the bondage of alcohol (see 1 Tim. 3:3; Titus 1:7).
- Not a bully. He is not physically violent and doesn't create trouble or look for fights (see 1 Tim. 3:3; Titus 1:7).
- Not quarrelsome. He is not given to selfish argumentation (see 1 Tim. 3:3).
- Gentle, fair, equitable, and does not insist on his own rights (see 1 Tim. 3:3)
- Not greedy. He is free from the love of money (see 1 Tim. 3:3; Titus 1:7).
- Manages his own household well, keeping his children under control with all dignity. He has the respect of his family and is recognized as the head/leader of his household (see 1 Tim. 3:4; Titus 1:6).
- Mature believer rather than a new convert. He has been a Christian long enough to demonstrate the reality of his conversion and the depth of his spirituality (see 1 Tim. 3:6).
- Good reputation among people outside the church. Unbelievers respect his character and integrity (1 Tim. 3:7).
- Not arrogant or stubborn. He does not insist on having his own way. He does not force his own ideas and opinions on others (see Titus 1:7).
- Not quick-tempered. He does not one fly off the handle or get angry quickly (see Titus 1:7).
- Loves what is good and wants to do God's will in everything (see Titus 1:8)
- Just, fair, impartial, and able to make objective judgments based on biblical principles (see Titus 1:8)
- Holds to the faithful message. He is committed to God's Word as true and authoritative, obedient to God's Word in all matters, not hypocritical but living in accordance with its teachings (see Titus 1:9).

God does not demand perfection in these areas, but He requires a heart commitment to His standards and a willingness to conform to them.

God does not demand perfection in these areas, but He requires a heart commitment to His standards and a willingness to conform to them. To serve as a spiritual leader in the church, a man must demonstrate a high degree of maturity and faithfulness in all of the areas listed above.

Compare the list of qualifications you made with your previous lists. Write down any qualifications that are not on your lists.

_____

_____

_____

_____

_____

_____

"Don't accept an accusation against an elder unless it is supported by two or three witnesses. Publicly rebuke those who sin, so that the rest will also be afraid."

1 Timothy 5:19-20

Accusations against or criticisms of spiritual leaders are to be received according to 1 Timothy 5:19-20. If a spiritual leader is guilty of an offense, he should be counseled by other godly, spiritually mature men with a view toward restoration (see Gal. 6:1-2). If he continues to sin, he should be removed from office and disciplined, according to Matthew 18:15-17. If a man is not above reproach, he is disqualified, in some cases permanently, from a position of leadership.[19] Restoration to fellowship does not always entail restoration to leadership. Spiritual integrity is crucial and nonnegotiable. If a spiritual leader is not guilty of something illegal, immoral, unethical, or clearly unbiblical, the church is responsible to follow his leadership, for this is the will of God (see 1 Thess. 5:12-15; Heb. 13:7,17).

HOW MANY SPIRITUAL LEADERS?

The argument for a plurality of spiritual leaders in a local congregation has significant biblical evidence. Every time the word *elder (presbuteros)* appears in the context of church leaders, it is always in the plural (see Acts 14:23; 16:4; 20:17; 21:18; 1 Tim. 5:17; Titus 1:5; Jas. 5:14; 1 Pet. 5:1). However, we believe the New Testament allows some degree of flexibility on this point. We believe the case for a single spiritual leader is biblically permissible. Several pieces of biblical evidence must be examined.

"Remember your leaders who have spoken God's word to you. As you carefully observe the outcome of their lives, imitate their faith. Obey your leaders and submit to them, for they keep watch over your souls as those who will give an account, so that they can do this with joy and not with grief, for that would be unprofitable for you."

Hebrews 13:7,17

Biblical models. The Bible never specifies a precise number of elders for a local congregation. Unlike the biblical teaching on congregationalism, which is quite clear, there is no corresponding evidence as to how many elders a church had, should have, or must have. Taking into consideration the reality of the house church in the early history of Christianity is important at this point. It is virtually certain that churches initially met in homes. At first they met in a single home,[20] but as the church grew and multiplied, more houses and elders were added.

The role of pastor-teacher. We should also take into account the reference to the pastor-teacher in Ephesians 4:11. It is extremely likely that the pastor-teacher is an elder, but the unique designation (pastor-teacher occurs only here) and context strongly suggest that this office is also distinctive within the category of elder. It has become popular for many churches to use the term *senior pastor.* Although the term itself does not appear in Scripture, the idea it conveys may reflect Ephesians 4:11.

Dever, himself an advocate of a plurality of elders, addresses this possibility: "If you ask the question, 'Does the Bible teach that there is to be a senior pastor-figure alongside, or inside the eldership?' we think the answer to that question is 'No, not directly.' Having said that, we do think that we *can* discern a distinct role among the elders for the one who is the primary public teacher of the church."[21] Though a senior elder is not identical to a single elder, there is certainly some similarity. If there is a plurality of elders, in essence the pastor-teacher is first among equals by virtue of his office and function among the elders.

In the Jerusalem conference in Acts 15 the role of a senior leader among the leaders emerges. James, Jesus' half-brother, was no monarchical bishop. He was with, of, and alongside the apostles and elders. Yet he was also above or over them as well. In Galatians Paul added evidence to the leadership position held by James in the church at Jerusalem (see 1:19; 2:9,12). This senior leader is no dictator or autocrat. He is accountable and responsible to the other leaders and to the congregation. Tragically, this point is something many pastors and churches neglect, and the churches of the Lord Jesus have suffered greatly as a result.

Scriptural qualifications for service. For those who lead the local body of Christ, the emphasis of Scripture is clear: leadership is based on spiritual qualifications for service. Men who are God-called, spiritually qualified, Spirit-gifted, and pastorally concerned are the only men who should be authorized to shepherd the flock of God. In some instances

Considerations in determining the number of elders:
- Biblical models
- Role of pastor-teacher
- Scriptural qualifications
- Giftedness

only one man may meet these qualifications. This fact in and of itself testifies to the legitimacy and acceptability of a single-elder model. This case would not be at all unusual in a church plant or start or even in a small church. At one time in America, as the gospel moved westward, pastors often ministered to multiple churches because of need and a shortage of God-called men. Quarter churches were congregations that had a circuit pastor-teacher who ministered once a month.[22] Was this an ideal arrangement? Of course not. Were they true churches nonetheless? Absolutely.

Where only one is qualified, God wants only one. As other men grow in their faith and meet the biblical requirements, they should join the work of ministry alongside and probably under the more mature minister who discipled them. We are convinced, based on the biblical evidence, that the number of elders is not the issue but that the nonnegotiable characteristic is whether church leaders meet scriptural qualifications. Because the elders give leadership and direction to the church, they must meet these biblical standards. Character and spiritual maturity are far more important than how many are responsible for this assignment.

Giftedness. Even a plurality-of-elders model allows room for a leader—a senior pastor, a pastor-teacher. It is absolutely essential that someone, by the moral integrity of his character and the gifts God has bestowed on him, take the lead in charting the church's direction. This is what 1 Timothy 5:17 intends when it says "an ample honorarium" is due those who "work hard at preaching and teaching." Such men give their lives to gospel ministry as their vocation and calling. They are not greater than others who are called by God and scripturally qualified, and yet they stand out as leaders among leaders. This is exactly the way many large churches with multiple staff members function.

The one deficiency we too often see in this model is the absence of an attitude of mutual submission (see Eph. 5:21), which requires the senior pastor to listen to and be accountable to the other ministers who serve with and under him. Fee provides a scathing critique on this issue:

> Although most Protestants in theory deny apostolic succession to reside in its clergy, *de facto* it is practiced in vigorous and sometimes devastating ways—in the "one-man show" of many denominational churches or in the little dictatorships in other (especially "independent") churches. And how did such a pluralism of papacies emerge? Basically from two

Character and spiritual maturity are far more important than how many are responsible for this assignment.

sources (not to mention the fallenness of the clergy whose egos often love such power): (a) from the fact that the local pastor is so often seen (and often sees himself …) as the authoritative interpreter of the "sole authority"—Scripture; (b) from the pastor's functioning in the role of authority, thus assuming the mantle of Paul or of a Timothy or Titus.[23]

In defending the allowance of a single-pastor model, we want to be clear that we are defending a particular form of the model, one that sees the necessity of and demand for mutual submission, respect, and accountability. There is no biblical defense for a dictatorial, autocratic, CEO model for ministry leadership. Pastors are shepherd-leaders—servant-leaders to the congregation and one another. One need only look to 3 John and the shameful example of a man named Diotrephes to see this autocratic pattern played out. It is not a pretty picture.[24] "Elders are to be other-centered. … As good shepherds, they are not to fleece the flock in self-interest but to tend and care for each of the sheep."[25] As gifted leaders, they lead. As God-called shepherds, they serve, even putting their lives on the line for the Savior's sheep if necessary. This is God's assignment for His undershepherds.

> **There is no biblical defense for a dictatorial, autocratic, CEO model for ministry leadership.**

DEACONS IN A NEW TESTAMENT CHURCH

As previously stated, the primary responsibility of spiritual leadership in a New Testament church is assigned to the pastor. Other leaders, according to Scripture, were deacons. Even though the seven in Acts 6:1-7 are not called deacons, that passage records the selection of the first men to serve alongside the apostles in the New Testament.

Read Acts 6:1-7. Then answer the following questions.

What problem arose in the early church (v. 1)? _____

_____

What solution did the twelve propose (vv. 2-4)? _____

_____

What were the qualifications for the seven men selected (v. 3)?

Who selected the seven men (vv. 3-6)?

What was the result of the church's actions (v. 7)?

The word *diakonos* is used in this passage as a verb meaning *to serve* and as a noun to refer to the ministry or service the men performed. Members of the church had a need: the Greek widows were hungry. Perhaps their families had disowned them when they became Christ-followers, or for some other reason they had no one to care for them. They likely spoke Greek, while the Jewish Christians spoke Aramaic. Ethnic tension had entered the church. The apostles cared enough to want the widows' needs to be met, but they also knew they must continue their focus on prayer, preaching, and evangelism.

The men chosen to distribute food to the widows were Greek men "of good reputation, full of the Spirit and wisdom, whom we can appoint to this duty" (Acts 6:3). The church approved of the plan (see v. 5), and the men chosen were set apart for service by the apostles, who prayed and laid their hands on them (v. 6).

Although the first responsibility of these seven men was to make sure the Greek widows received food in the daily distribution, we know they were also preachers and evangelists. Stephen was performing great wonders and signs among the people when he was accused of blasphemy and martyred (see Acts 6:8; 7:59). Philip was also known as a preacher and an evangelist (see Acts 8:5-12,26-40). In fact, deacons in the New Testament performed a wide range of ministries. It is clear from this biblical example that the role of deacon is one of servant to the church. The appointed men brought harmony in the church fellowship; ministered to the church's physical, emotional, and spiritual needs; and led the church in spiritual growth and maturity.[26]

Diakonos *(Greek):* **to serve; ministry or service**

The role of deacon is one of servant to the church.

"Deacons, likewise, should be worthy of respect, not hypocritical, not drinking a lot of wine, not greedy for money, holding the mystery of the faith with a clear conscience. And they must also be tested first; if they prove blameless, then they can serve as deacons. Wives, too, must be worthy of respect, not slanderers, self-controlled, faithful in everything. Deacons must be husbands of one wife, managing their children and their own households competently. For those who have served well as deacons acquire a good standing for themselves, and great boldness in the faith that is in Christ Jesus.

1 Timothy 3:8-13

In Philippians 1:1 deacons and pastors are mentioned together: "Paul and Timothy, slaves of Christ Jesus: to all the saints in Christ Jesus who are in Philippi, including the overseers and deacons." Paul's instructions to the churches about the type of men who should be deacons establishes deacons as leaders in the New Testament churches (see 1 Tim. 3:8-13), and many requirements for deacons are the same as those of elders.

PRACTICAL IMPLICATIONS OF NEW TESTAMENT CHURCH GOVERNMENT

Based on our study of New Testament patterns, we can draw several conclusions about the way a church is to be organized.

1. Congregationalism is the form of church government modeled and practiced in the New Testament.

2. Congregationalism honors the doctrine of the priesthood of believers and the church as the body of Christ. It recognizes the fact that God calls each believer to doctrinal vigilance and that God gifts every believer for service to the body. It recognizes that God has committed certain matters to the congregation as a whole.

3. Congregationalism functions effectively only within the context of a regenerate church membership that practices church discipline. If these two essential pillars of polity are not honored and consistently practiced, unbelieving, carnal persons will influence the affairs of the church, with devastating consequences.

4. Congregationalism may follow a representative model. The church should seek, call, and follow godly leaders. We should willingly and joyfully submit to their direction and leadership (see 1 Thess. 5:12-13; Heb. 13:7,17,24).

5. Calling and following God-called leaders does not mean those leaders are not accountable both to God and to

the congregation. Leaders also need close, inner-circle accountability as well. This is especially important where the single-pastor model is practiced. Carson points out that ironically, some forms of congregationalism elevate the pastor, once he has been voted in, to near papal authority, in practice if not in theory.[27] Whether you call them elders, overseers, or pastors, they all need accountability with those who love them enough to speak the truth in love (see Eph. 4:15), even when it hurts. There is no place for pride in the Christian life. There is no place for a Lone Ranger approach to ministry. Leaders need others who can encourage them and hold them accountable. This is especially true for the shepherd who watches over God's flock. All of us have weaknesses, blind spots, and areas of deficiency. A counsel of godly men around a minister, in some form, is absolutely essential for his health and safety.

6. Although there must be accountability, we must also affirm the God-ordained mandate to let God-called leaders lead. Whether their number is one, a few, or many, they are to be loved, respected, and followed in recognition of God's gifts and calling in their lives. Following church leaders, however, does not imply blind loyalty. If a pastor does something unbiblical, immoral, illegal, or unethical, we are biblically obligated to confront him and to follow the pattern of 1 Timothy 5:19-20. If we disagree with a decision he makes, the direction he provides, or a judgment he renders, we have the right to go to him and share our concern. But having done this, we are then to support his leadership. Why? Because he is the God-called leader of the church, and we are not. God tells us to remember (pray for), obey, and submit to our pastor because he (1) watches over our soul and (2) must give an account to God (see Heb. 13:7,17). God wants pastors to serve the congregation with joy, not grief. We do our part to ensure this by obeying and submitting. This mind-set is foreign to our radically autonomous, democratic, and egalitarian culture. However, it is clearly biblical, and we ignore or

God tells us to remember (pray for), obey, and submit to our pastor.

disobey God's command on this point only to our shame and loss (see Heb. 13:17b).

7. Strong pastoral leadership is essential to the growth and maturation of the church.[28] Churches that are growing numerically and spiritually accept and follow strong leadership. This is not surprising, given the fact that this model for church and ministry is established in Scripture.

8. The late Adrian Rogers, the former pastor of Bellevue Baptist Church in Memphis, Tennessee, said with characteristic wit, "Anything without a head is dead. Anything with several heads is a freak." That is a colorful way of recognizing the fact that someone has to lead. Though many may give counsel, provide input, and share wisdom, a leader must be out front leading the way. Because the church and the ministry are spiritual in nature, consensus should always be the goal, especially among the pastor and staff. "My way or the highway" is not biblical.

9. Finally, we could personally pastor a church with a single pastor, a church with co-pastors, or a church with an official plurality of elders. Why? Because quite simply, we believe the New Testament allows such flexibility in church polity. In each model we would seek to guide, not drive; lead, not dictate. We would establish, where it is not already in place, an accountable relationship with other godly men so that we could safely and effectively discharge our duties as ministers of Jesus Christ. This practice is biblical, wise, and essential for the church's health and well-being. We would follow a shepherd model as we lead God's flock, and in all things we would strive for the glory of God (see 1 Cor. 10:31). Yet it is possible to get the structure right and still miss the mark if the Spirit of Christ is absent. Clowney is right when he says, "Even the best form of church government is an empty shell if these principles [Christ's headship, the church as the organic life of His body, and the principles of service and stewardship

guiding the leadership] do not grip the hearts of those who lead and those who follow. Better by far are imperfect structures in the hands of devoted servants of Christ than the most biblical form of church government practiced in pride or in a loveless and vindictive spirit."[29]

THE IMPERFECT LOCAL CHURCH

"Well, I found at least one encouraging part of this study," Mark reflected to Jim. "All the scholars tell us that no local church is perfect in its organization. But I have to admit, I am discouraged how far from the biblical model our church is. During our study I made a list of some of the areas in which we have fallen short:

- "We had one pastor who was totally authoritarian. I guess the church was right in addressing his dictatorial approach. But I'm not sure we handled the situation scripturally.
- "The pastor-search committee overreacted by recommending the next pastor, who was not a leader at all. Nothing got done because no one was responsible for leadership.
- "The church overreacted in that same situation by putting together a cumbersome committee system that does not allow for pastoral leadership.
- "Our business meetings are now little more than family fights. We rarely discuss things that really matter.

"The time our church was healthiest was when we had a godly pastor and staff. Although we have never had elders, our staff acted the way plural leadership is supposed to act, and our deacons were truly a servant body instead of a corporate board. The pastor and staff were accountable to the congregation, and the congregation respected and followed their leadership. After completing this study, I now realize that we were organized mostly along New Testament teachings. Maybe I can be an influence to move our church back in that direction."

"Good enough," Jim responded. "Let's see, the next area we said we would study is the topic of church discipline."

"Oh, great," Mark laughed. "I think I might get depressed again."

"The time our church was healthiest was when we had a godly pastor and staff."

[Q] Review your memory verses for this chapter.

Based on what you have learned in this chapter, identify some needs your pastor and deacons may have that church members can help to meet.

Your pastor: _____

_____

_____

_____

Your deacons: _____

_____

_____

_____

What are two ways you can better support your pastor and deacons?

1. _____

_____

2. _____

_____

What two actions can you take to show your appreciation
for your pastor and deacons?

1. _____

_____

2. _____

_____

🔍 Spend some time in prayer for your pastor and deacons.
Thank God for them and for their ministry. Pray that
God will guide them as they lead and serve your church.
Pray about the needs you listed on the previous page.

HOW DOES A VIBRANT CHURCH MAKE DECISIONS?

BEFORE THE SESSION

1. Study chapter 3 and complete the learning activities.
2. Write the following Scripture references on separate index cards.
    - Group 1: *Matthew 18:15-17*
    - Group 2: *Acts 6:1-7*
    - Group 3: *Acts 11:19-26*
    - Group 4: *Acts 14:26-28*
    - Group 5: *Acts 15:1-35. Give attention to verses 1-4,12,22-23,30.*
3. Prepare four group-assignment slips.
    - Group 1: *Study Acts 20:17-38 and prepare a job description for a pastor, based on Paul's example.*
    - Group 2: *Study 1 Timothy 3:1-7 and identify the qualifications for a pastor.*
    - Group 3: *Read Titus 1:5-9 and identify the qualifications for a pastor.*
    - Group 4: *Read 1 Peter 5:1-4 and identify the qualifications for a pastor.*

DURING THE SESSION

1. Refer to the title of chapter 3. Ask a volunteer to lead in prayer.
2. Define the five types of church government discussed on pages 59–60. Write the name of each type on a dry-erase board as you introduce it. Give examples of denominations or groups that practice each form.
3. Define *congregationalism* and direct attention to the true/false activity on page 61. Lead the group to respond to and discuss the statements. Ask any members who have been affiliated with other denominations to briefly describe differences they noticed between that form of government and congregational church government.
4. Divide into five small groups and give each group one of the cards with Scripture references. Each the groups to read their assigned Scriptures and to be prepared to report on the ways their Scriptures support congregationalism. Allow time for work and call for reports.

5. Review the definitions of *priesthood of believers, soul competency,* and *religious liberty* on pages 67–68. Lead a discussion of each concept and explain the implications for congregational church government.

6. Direct attention to the true/false activity on page 67. Lead the group to respond to and discuss the statements.

7. Ask for a volunteer to explain the difference between *the priesthood of the believer* and *the priesthood of all believers* (see p. 68).

8. Write on a dry-erase board: *poimen, presbuteros, episkopos.* Explain the terms *pastor, elder,* and *bishop.* Make sure members understand that the three terms are interchangeable, and the New Testament uses all three for the same office. Use Acts 20:17-31 in your explanation.

9. Ask volunteers to describe ways your pastor cares for and feeds your congregation. Ask how his administrative role is reflected as he leads your church. Ask how his wisdom and maturity are reflected as he guides your church.

10. Divide members into four groups and give each group an assignment slip. Allow time for work; then call for the three reports on the qualifications for a pastor. Ask a volunteer to write the qualifications on a dry-erase board as they are identified. Ask for the report on a pastor's job description. Ask a volunteer to write the qualifications on the dry-erase board.

11. Direct attention to the responsibilities of a pastor on pages 74–75. Ask a volunteer to read these aloud.

12. Share that the other leaders in New Testament churches were deacons. Direct attention to the Bible-study activity on pages 80–81. Ask a volunteer to read Acts 6:1-7. Ask members to answer the questions in the activity.

13. Direct attention to 1 Timothy 3:8-13. Ask members to identify the requirements for deacons as a volunteer records them on a dry-erase board.

14. Summarize the session by using selected remarks in the section "Practical Implications of New Testament Church Government," beginning on page 82. Ask members to cite examples of the exercise of congregational church government in their church. Ask: *What are the advantages of congregationalism? What are some pitfalls, and how can they be avoided?*

15. Call on volunteers to recite the memory verses from chapters 1 and 2. As a group, read aloud the memory verses for chapter 3.

16. Ask members to share ways by they can better support and show appreciation to their pastor and deacons.

17. Close with prayer for your pastor and deacons. Thank God for them and for their ministry. Pray that God will guide them as they lead and serve the church.

Chapter 4

DOES MY CHURCH HAVE TO PRACTICE CHURCH DISCIPLINE?

Learning Goals

A study of this chapter will raise your awareness of the subject of church discipline and the basic Bible teachings on the subject. You will develop sensitivity to the need and process of church discipline, and you will be motivated to pray for the health and corporate witness of your church as a whole.

Memory Verses

"Brothers, if someone is caught in any wrongdoing, you who are spiritual should restore such a person with a gentle spirit, watching out for yourselves so you won't be tempted also. Carry one another's burdens; in this way you will fulfill the law of Christ" (Gal. 6:1-2).

"I have to admit," Mark told Jim, "I've attended church all of my life, and I doubt that I know more than you do about church discipline. I have never studied it, nor have I ever seen a church practice it."

Jim responded, "Well, we have gathered this wealth of books and other material on the church, and the issue of church discipline comes up again and again. One book says the healthiest churches have high expectations of its members. And it also says a church with high expectations must have a biblical method in place to deal with members who stray from God's plan for them."

"You know," Mark said thoughtfully, "I've heard of a few churches that attempted to practice church discipline, but the result was a church fight and a church split. I wonder how my church can practice discipline without tearing the congregation apart."

"It sounds as if it's time for our study to begin," Mark answered. So the two men opened their books and their Bibles.

THE BIBLICAL FOUNDATIONS OF CHURCH DISCIPLINE

A local church learns that one of its deacons has left his wife and children and is living with another woman. The pastor, as a good shepherd of "God's flock among you" (1 Pet. 5:2), goes to see this man with Galatians 6:1-2 beating in his heart and Jesus' words in Matthew 18:15 as his guide. The man living in sin, however, is unrepentant and will not heed his pastor's counsel to forsake his sin. The pastor commits to pray for this deacon and invites other leaders in the church to do the same.

The pastor waits several months and then follows the next step Jesus specified: he takes two other Christian brothers and once more confronts this man about his sin (see Matt. 18:16). Again, he is rebuffed, this time with anger. The sinning man informs these three Christian brothers that he has no intention of leaving his sin and seeking reconciliation with his wife and children. Heartbroken, the pastor and his Christian brothers commit themselves to pray even more fervently for this man whom they love and have known for many years as a faithful servant of Christ.

After several more months they go to him again but with no success. In fact, the man tells them not to come back, that he does not wish to see or hear from them again.

"If your brother sins against you, go and rebuke him in private. If he listens to you, you have won your brother. But if he won't listen, take one or two more with you, so that by the testimony of two or three witnesses every fact may be established. If he pays no attention to them, tell the church. But if he doesn't pay attention even to the church, let him be like an unbeliever and a tax collector to you."

Matthew 18:15-17

At this point the pastor follows the third step Jesus outlined: he brings the situation to the church and calls the whole body to a season of intercession for this unrepentant deacon. He encourages those who know him well to call, write, or visit him. This continues for several more months, but there is still no repentance. Finally, following Jesus' command (see Matt. 18:17) and Paul's directive (see 1 Cor. 5:1-13), church leaders make plans to remove this man from church membership and its privileges, although he is still welcome to attend services in hopes that hearing the Word of God will bring conviction and repentance. But he will no longer be considered a member in good standing.

When these plans are presented to the church, there is an explosive, visceral reaction by a vocal group in the church. This group accuses the pastor and other church leaders of being unloving and judgmental. Members of the group state that this man has the right to be a church member and that what he does in his private life is no one's business. Extended family members of the man are embarrassed and scandalized that the pastor is proposing such a radical and seemingly unloving action.

The phones start ringing, and private meetings are held. Persons who have not attended the church for years but are still on the rolls are called for support against the pastor. Sadly and tragically, the sinning man is not removed from church membership. The pastor is terminated, and the godly leadership in the church resigns. The church's reputation is severely damaged on a number of fronts. In heaven our Lord's heart is broken over His people's blatant disobedience to His Word. This story is not fictional. It is true. Names are withheld to protect the guilty!

The pastor attempted to follow Jesus' teachings on church discipline. Read Matthew 18:15-17 and state the four steps in church discipline outlined in this passage.

1. _____

2. _____

3. _____

4. _____

Although many church members today might be uncomfortable with the concept of church discipline, the New Testament has a great deal to say about it. Jesus addressed the topic in Matthew 18:15-20, and Paul repeatedly did so in Romans 16:17-18; 1 Corinthians 5:1-13; 2 Corinthians 2:5-11; 13:1-3; Galatians 6:1-2; 2 Thessalonians 3:6-12; and Titus 3:9-15.

Read each Scripture passage and match it with the correct summary statement.

_____ 1. Matthew 18:15

_____ 2. Romans 16:17-18

_____ 3. 1 Corinthians 5:1-2

_____ 4. 1 Corinthians 5:9-10

_____ 5. 2 Corinthians 2:5-11

_____ 6. Hebrews 12:5-6

a. Sexual immorality in the church should be dealt with.

b. Avoid persons who create dissensions.

c. God disciplines His children.

d. Jesus commanded church discipline.

e. When a believer repents of his sin, the church should reach out to him in love and forgiveness.

f. Church discipline does not apply to non-Christians.

Answers: 1. d, 2. b, 3. a, 4. f, 5. e, 6. c

Despite the presence of so many Scripture passages on the subject, no aspect of church life in our day is more neglected than this one. Indeed, the church's disregard for this clear teaching of Holy Scripture is perhaps its greatest visible act of disobedience to our Lord. This rebellion is not without significant consequences. John L. Dagg cogently noted, "When discipline leaves a church, Christ goes with it."[1] Mark Dever, building on the biblical theme that God's people must reflect His character, wrote, "In the New Testament, the church is also to exercise discipline, because an expectation of holiness remains upon God's people."[2]

Baptists' neglect of this teaching is striking when you consider that we have historically viewed church discipline as an essential mark of the church, right alongside the Word rightly preached and the ordinances properly administered. Al Mohler notes that the inclusion of discipline as an essential mark of the church "goes back at least to the Belgic Confession of 1561,"[3] and we can also find the roots of this practice in the earliest Anabaptist Confession, the Schleitheim Confession of 1527, in article 2 on the Ban.[4]

> The church's disregard for this clear teaching of Holy Scripture is perhaps its greatest visible act of disobedience to our Lord.

Yet none of our most recent statements of faith, *The Baptist Faith and Message* 1925, 1963, and 2000, include a statement on this biblical teaching. There are probably several reasons, and they may seem legitimate to some. Greg Wills points out that church discipline began to wane in Southern Baptist life in the 1870s and rapidly declined thereafter. "By the 1930s discipline was quite rare—most reported exclusions were merely the cleaning of church rolls of names of members long inactive and forgotten."[5] Of course, today we seldom do even this. Clearly, we have a problem that needs to be addressed.

Why do you think Baptists in recent years have neglected church discipline?

_____

_____

Compare your response with the following paragraphs.

> "Husbands, love your wives, just as also Christ loved the church and gave Himself for her, to make her holy, cleansing her in the washing of water by the word. He did this to present the church to Himself in splendor, without spot or wrinkle or any such thing, but holy and blameless."
>
> Ephesians 5:25-27

How did we get to a place where the "people of the Book" show such disregard for a clear command of Christ and a crucial component of church life? Certainly, there have been abuses of the practice in the past, though memories of these are far removed from our own day. No, we have been seduced in a far more insidious fashion. Wills notes factors like "urbanization, faith in moral and social progress, civil religion, activism … the search for church efficiency … [and] commitment to an expansive individualism" as undermining our "commitment to the authority of the congregation."[6]

We agree with Wills's assessment, though we prefer to address the situation in practical and spiritual terms. We believe the genesis of the disease is fourfold. In each instance the problem often finds its origin at the top with the pastoral leadership.

A loss of theological nerve. We no longer have the courage to confront as well as comfort, to admonish as well as exhort. From a fear of offending, we have slinked away into the false security of silence.

Compromised morality. We have far too many morally sick and anemic churches. So many of our congregations look and act like the world that we would hardly know where to begin if we restored church discipline. The purity of the bride of Christ (see Eph. 5:25-27) is noticeably absent.

Biblical illiteracy. Lay this deficiency at the feet of pastors who have jettisoned an expository model of preaching, allowing churches to avoid and neglect the hard doctrines of Scripture like church discipline. In addition, far too many churches fail to systematically teach biblical doctrine to their members through a corporate discipleship strategy.

Practical expediency. Practical expediency and denominational ambition sometimes play an all-too-important role in church life. A bigger membership means greater bragging rights and affords a more attractive platform, so churches are reluctant to drop people from their rolls. Furthermore, Southern Baptists' fascination with and fixation on numbers naturally enslave us to this mind-set. Numbers and an accurate accounting of those numbers are important. Keeping good records is wise and responsible. It is a matter of accountability and integrity. It is even biblical (see Acts 2:41). However, if we inflate, exaggerate, and become infatuated with numbers, we can take the focus off God's intended purpose for the church, thereby dishonoring Christ, robbing the church of integrity, and calling into question the church's credibility.

Causes for the neglect of church discipline:
- **Loss of theological nerve**
- **Compromised morality**
- **Biblical illiteracy**
- **Practical expediency**

Match the following statements with the four terms used to explain our neglect of church discipline.

____ 1. We have failed to teach the whole counsel of God.

____ 2. We do not want to offend people.

____ 3. We want to keep our membership roll as large as possible.

____ 4. Worldliness has crept into the congregation.

a. A loss of theological nerve

b. Compromised morality

c. Biblical illiteracy

d. Practical expediency

"Those who accepted his message were baptized, and that day about 3,000 people were added to them."

Acts 2:41

Where, then, do we turn for a solution to this critical condition in which we find the modern church? Wanting to model what we believe is the way out and the way forward, we will direct our attention to a particular Scripture text that addresses church discipline. It will provide a foundation for a general understanding of this issue, as well as specific counsel for particular situations that demand the exercise of church discipline.

The text, Titus 3:9-15, was written in the context of a church-planting movement on the island of Crete (see Titus 1:5). Thus, from a church's

Answers: 1. c, 2. a, 3. d, 4. b

inception Paul believed a disciplined membership was an essential and necessary mark. Here Paul provided five principles by which the body of Christ is to conduct the practice of church discipline. We will complement his teachings with insights from other passages as well.

AVOID THE FOOLISH (TITUS 3:9)

"Avoid foolish debates, genealogies, quarrels, and disputes about the law, for they are unprofitable and worthless."

Titus 3:9

This epistle contains Paul's final words to his son in the ministry, Titus. Like the constant beating of a drum, Paul repeatedly challenged those at Crete to maintain sound doctrine and good works.

It is essential that a church protect and value its doctrinal and moral integrity. Those who would compromise in either area must be confronted and, if unrepentant, avoided. To do so is loving. Not to do so is to mistake sentimentality for love. Victor Masters understood this well when he wrote, "Sentimentality is an enemy of church discipline. Sentimentality is the love of man divorced from love of truth. ... It cloaks a big lot of hypocrisy and moral decay."[7]

Paul said to avoid the foolish. The word *avoid* can be translated *shun*. It is a present imperative, a word of command, calling for constant and consistent vigilance. Why must we avoid, shun, turn away from these kind of people? Two reasons are given.

The foolish are unwise. Paul described these troublemakers first as those who engage in "foolish debates [NIV, 'controversies'], genealogies, quarrels [NIV, 'arguments'], and disputes about the law." In this context the troublemakers were Judaizers, who added to both the words of Scripture and the work of our Savior. They debated theological minutiae, created fanciful allegories and mythologies based on biblical genealogies, and added works to the doctrine of salvation by grace alone through faith alone in Christ alone.

Judaizers:

Jewish Christians in the first century who tried to convince Gentile Christians that they needed to conform to the law of Moses

Paul described the troublemakers more fully in Titus 1:10-14. Read this passage and answer the following questions.

What are the three ways these troublemakers are described (v. 10)?

What was their influence on families in the church (v. 11)?

What was their motive in teaching (v. 11)?

How did a Cretan poet describe Cretans (v. 12)?

What did Paul command Titus to do (v. 13)?

What was to be the purpose in confronting the troublemakers (vv. 13-14)?

Principles for practicing church discipline:
- **Avoid the foolish.**
- **Reject the divisive.**
- **Follow the leader.**
- **Maintain good works.**
- **Enlist the faithful.**

"If someone is caught in any wrongdoing, you who are spiritual should restore such a person with a gentle spirit, watching out for yourselves so you won't be tempted also. Carry one another's burdens; in this way you will fulfill the law of Christ."

Galatians 6:1-2

Thinking of themselves as the theological elite, the Judaizers tore up and would continue to tear up "whole households" (Titus 1:11) if left unchecked. These kinds of persons are not to be debated but denounced and dismissed. Dealing with aberrant theology is not the time for dialogue. It is the time for swift action. False theology always requires quick and decisive church discipline.

The foolish are unprofitable. Going beyond Scripture; adding to the work of Christ; and advocating a Jesus-plus, faith-plus, and Word-plus theological agenda make these false teachers unprofitable and worthless. Nothing good comes from their attitude or their teachings. The goal of avoiding them is to bring to light their error and their sin. It is redemptive and restorative (see Gal. 6:1-2). It is essential and not optional. Even one evangelist of error is one too many. The risks are too great.

REJECT THE DIVISIVE (TITUS 3:10-11)

Refusing to enter unnecessary theological wrangling does not mean inaction. As the stakes rise, we must respond. Paul in essence summarized Jesus' teachings on church discipline found in Matthew 18:15-17. Carefully note the sin that must be confronted: it is public, habitual, serious, and lacking repentance. These four criteria are at the heart of a biblical theology of church discipline.

We are not called to be spiritual garbage inspectors or theological peeping toms. When we become aware of a sinning brother or sister, we first go to them individually and second with witnesses. If there is no repentance, we finally take the matter to the whole fellowship.

If at any point evidence of genuine repentance comes forth, the process of discipline stops, and the ministry of restoration begins. This is always the desired goal. Parenthetically, restoration to fellowship does not always entail restoration to leadership. God's standard for the latter is higher than His standard for the former.

The ministry of church discipline is mandatory if we are to be faithful to our head, who is Christ. We do it for the sake of the body and for the sake of the sinning brother. Dietrich Bonhoeffer emphasized the crucial nature of discipline when he wrote, "Nothing can be more cruel than the tenderness that consigns another to his sin. Nothing can be more compassionate than that severe rebuke that calls a brother back from the path of sin."[8]

> *If evidence of genuine repentance comes forth, the process of discipline stops, and the ministry of restoration begins.*

State four criteria for sin that must be confronted.
If you need help, review the previous paragraphs.

1. _____
2. _____
3. _____
4. _____

> Answers: public, habitual, serious, and lacking repentance

The primary goal of church discipline is (check the correct response)—

___ 1. to excommunicate the sinning person from the church;

___ 2. to serve as a warning to the church as a whole;

___ 3. to restore the sinning person to fellowship with Christ and the church;

___ 4. to show unbelievers that the church will not tolerate sin.

> Answer: 3

Explain Bonhoeffer's statement in your own words: "Nothing can be more compassionate than that severe rebuke that calls a brother back from the path of sin."

Paul made three helpful observations about the divisive.

The divisive must be disciplined (Titus 3:10). *Reject* (NIV, "warn") is another command. *Divisive* is the Greek word *hairetikos*, from which we get our word *heretic*.[9] However, its first-century meaning referred to "a person who is quarrelsome and stirs up factions through erroneous opinions, a man who is determined to go his own way and so forms parties and factions."[10] This is the man who, as John MacArthur says, "is a law to himself and has no concern for spiritual truth or unity."[11]

Paul's instructions are clear: admonish him once; admonish him twice. If there is no repentance, he must be rejected. Dever points out, "The nature of the exclusion Paul enjoined [here and in texts like 1 Cor. 5] is excommunication, which typically means excluding the parties in question from communion (the Lord's Supper). In essence, this is a removal from church membership."[12]

Dealing with such an individual in this manner has pastoral benefits. It keeps the issue on the level of principle and not personality. Personality battles result when we delay in taking action and are perceived to show favoritism. This is always a lose-lose scenario and must be avoided. We must move quickly in the initial stage when the sin is discovered. We may extend the grace of patience as we seek the repentance of the person living in sin. However, we must be clear, straightforward, and timely. We cannot go to the person once and then, if there is no change, walk away as if all is forgiven. We must also be vigilant and steadfast, all the while keeping Galatians 6:1-2 in mind.

The divisive are dangerous (Titus 3:11). Why must habitual, public, serious, unrepentant sinners be disciplined? Because they are dangerous. Paul said such a person is perverted and sins. *Perverted* literally means *twisted, turned inside out. Sins* is in the present tense. The person is described as living life upside down and inside out. This is his settled state, heart, and mind—his continuous habit of life.

"Reject a divisive person after a first and second warning, knowing that such a person is perverted and sins, being self-condemned."

Titus 3:10-11

Paul certainly did something when it came to public, habitual, serious, and unrepented sin in Corinth and here on Crete! Again Bonhoeffer's wisdom comes to center stage: "Reproof is unavoidable. God's Word demands it when a brother falls into open sin."[13] We do neither the sinner nor ourselves any favors when we ignore a sin that is dangerous and destroys.

The divisive are destructive (Titus 3:11). Sin is destructive. It destroys. What it can do to a fellowship is serious. What it does to the sinner enslaved by its addiction is tragic. *Self-condemned* in this passage is an interesting word. The Greek word is *autokatakritos*, which means *to judge down on oneself,* hence to be self-condemned. In action and attitude the sinner is without excuse, passing judgment on himself. He may not see it, for he is warped, twisted, and self-deceived. He may even attempt to use Scripture to justify his sin. Often he claims the leading of the Spirit and sometimes even the providence of God. Sometimes he may even say, "My head tells me this is wrong, but my heart tells me it was never more right."

With grief, humility, self-examination, and a broken heart we must confront the divisive person.

With grief, humility, self-examination, and a broken heart we must confront the divisive person and, if necessary, shun him and reject him. Following Paul's directive in 1 Corinthians 5:1-13, we must turn him over to Satan with a hope and a prayer that the discipline of the Heavenly Father (see Heb. 12:5-13) will bring him to brokenness and repentance and that he will give evidence that he is indeed God's child. We have our duty. God has His. We must do our part. God will always do His.

Read 1 Corinthians 5. Choose the best response to complete each of the following statements.

1. The sin in the church at Corinth was—
   ○ a. sexual immorality;
   ○ b. doctrinal error;
   ○ c. idolatry.

2. The attitude of the church toward the sinning person was—
   ○ a. indifference;
   ○ b. pride and boasting;
   ○ c. sorrow and concern.

3. To turn the sinning person over to Satan was Paul's way of saying—
   ○ a. to stop praying for the person;
   ○ b. to pray that the person will seek forgiveness;
   ○ c. to excommunicate the person from the church.

Answers: 1. a, 2. b, 3. c

FOLLOW THE LEADER (TITUS 3:12-13)

Verses 12-15 are Paul's final words to Titus. Their proximity to verses 9-11 and the instructions found in them suggest that the words not only provide a farewell message but also amplify Paul's teaching on church discipline. The counsel we discover helps to guide us through the difficult waters of church discipline.

Good, godly leadership is absolutely essential if a church is to carry out the ministry of loving confrontation. Such leadership must be in place, respected, trusted, and evident to the congregation. This leadership should be visible among the pastoral staff as well as among the laity. Church discipline is no place for a Lone Ranger. Going solo in this arena is unbiblical. Following the leader means there is a leader. It means establishing credibility and earning the right to be followed in doing the difficult work of the church. When you have that, you can act decisively and courageously.

Each church must establish its own process for church discipline. This should include a plan for teaching members what the Bible says about discipline, as well as why, when, and for what reasons the church-discipline process will be implemented. A church should follow biblical guidelines, determine who will be involved in exercising church discipline, and establish the precise steps that will be followed. Some of these functions and roles may be specified in your church's constitution and bylaws. In addition, the church may want to collect questions that are raised about church discipline: Who can receive church discipline? Who will implement it? Who will know the details? What happens if the person does not repent or change? What happens if the person repents and changes? What will the process be? After questions are collected, ensure that the answers are part of the church's process for carrying out discipline.

Titus 3 addresses the church body's role in church discipline.

The church must listen to leaders' advice (Titus 3:12). In the midst of great challenge and controversy, Paul stepped forward and made important decisions that affected numerous lives and ensured the continuation of necessary church ministries. Paul would relieve Titus of his responsibilities on Crete by sending Artemas, of whom we know nothing, or Tychicus, of whom we know quite a bit. Griffin informs us that Tychicus was "Paul's traveling companion (see Acts 20:4), 'dear brother and faithful servant in the Lord' (see Ephesians 6:21; Colossians 4:7), and his personal representative to churches (see 2 Timothy 4:12)."[14]

"When I send Artemas to you, or Tychicus, make every effort to come to me in Nicopolis, for I have decided to spend the winter there. Diligently help Zenas the lawyer and Apollos on their journey, so that they will lack nothing."

Titus 3:12-13

Both men must have been capable of fulfilling Paul's instructions in 3:10-11, or he would not have sent them. This would free Titus to go to Nicopolis (meaning "city of victory"; nine such cities existed in New Testament times)[15] on the western coast of Achaia or in the southern province of Greece. Paul would go there for the winter to rest, strategize, and spend time with Titus. Because Paul would send godly, spiritual reinforcements who could handle any more troublemakers if they should arise, Titus could set aside this work and move ahead to a new ministry that would soon take him to Dalmatia (see 2 Tim. 4:9).

The church must assist in the process of church discipline (Titus 3:13). Church discipline should not be the primary focal point of the church's ministry. Its necessity and practice should not require the neglect of other vital activities. In fact, we believe Paul envisioned it as a natural component of the very fabric of the church's identity and mission, a painful but essential aspect of Christian discipleship. Paul could instruct Titus on the principles of church discipline, at the same time giving attention to other ministries that needed to be carried out. In all of this he needed the help of others, and they gladly assisted their trusted leader.

Zenas the lawyer (the only Christian lawyer noted in all of the New Testament, probably a Roman jurist in our judgment) and Apollos (the eloquent Alexandrian who came onstage in Acts 18–19 and was highly revered in Corinth) were apparently with Titus on Crete. No doubt they had assisted him in the ministry of church discipline. Now their services were needed elsewhere, since the discipline matters at Crete were under control. Titus should send them on quickly, making sure "that they will lack nothing."

Church discipline is a natural dimension of the multifaceted ministries of church life. It is not preeminent, but neither should it be an anomaly. **The church exercises discipline as a matter of Christian discipleship and ongoing responsibility to ensure the health and vibrancy of the body of Christ.**

> **The church exercises discipline as a matter of Christian discipleship and ongoing responsibility to ensure the health and vibrancy of the body of Christ.**

MAINTAIN GOOD WORKS (TITUS 3:14)

Good works are a reoccurring theme throughout this short, three-chapter, 46-verse letter. The phrase occurs six times, driving home the point that though we are not saved by faith plus works (see Eph. 2:8-10; Titus 3:5), we are saved by a faith that works. The presence and practice of these

good works provide a context for the healthy practice of church discipline. Furthermore, one of the good works that characterizes a healthy congregation is church discipline.

In verse 14 Paul says good works must not be neglected. Good works, including the good works of 3:9-10, are to be our habits of life. They are the norm and not the exception, for to neglect them is to function as a substandard, below-the-bar church. Tony Evans is on target in saying, "A church that does not practice discipline of its members is not functioning properly as a church, just as a family that does not discipline is not a fully functioning family."[16]

The good work of church discipline will meet the need and bear the fruit of—

- the glory of God;
- love for the sinner;
- restoration of the wayward;
- the purity of the church;
- the protection of the fellowship;
- a witness to the world.

"Our people must also learn to devote themselves to good works for cases of urgent need, so that they will not be unfruitful."

Titus 3:14

Church discipline is a good work of duty and necessity. Avoiding the ever-present sins of legalism and judgmentalism, we testify to God, one another, and the world that holiness and purity matter. We proclaim through biblical discipline that love cares and confronts. It can be tender, but it can also be tough. What it cannot do is stand by and do nothing when a member of the body is snared by sin. We do not discipline the world and have no mandate from our Lord to do so. To them we proclaim the gospel of Jesus Christ. It is among ourselves that we practice the ministry of loving confrontation. As the revivalist Charles Finney wrote, "If you see your neighbor sin, and you pass by and neglect to reprove him, it is just as cruel as if you should see his house on fire, and pass by and not warn him of it."[17] Good works indeed meet urgent needs.

How can a church that practices church discipline avoid the sins of legalism and judgmentalism?

How can church discipline be tender?

How can church discipline be tough?

ENLIST THE FAITHFUL (TITUS 3:15)

This final verse is a farewell statement from friends to friends. It is all-encompassing. Subtly and just beneath the surface, we find two words of wisdom for the life and ministry of confrontation: *love* and *grace*. Those whose lives are characterized by these twin towers of the Christian life are qualified for the hard task and difficult assignment of church discipline. Paul addressed these Christian companions by means of a personal greeting and a prayer.

All who were with Paul expressed their greeting to and love for Titus. Like Paul, they knew the challenges he faced; and they wanted him to know they cared, stood with him, and were on his side. This assurance could only encourage him in the tough task of church discipline. As those of the same faith, they were one with him in the battle.

Bitterness is an ever-present enemy to those in the ministry. This is especially the case when we are called to the ministry of discipline and restoration. Only God's grace will give us balance, self-control, wisdom, and endurance. By God's grace and for God's glory we will be equipped and enabled to stand and serve, even when the odds are against us and the battle seems all for nothing.

The battle we fight is the Lord's! His amazing grace is what we need when the fire is hot or the water is deep. Such is often our lot in the ministry of confrontation. At such times only His grace will sustain us. Amazingly, we will discover that it is all we need.

PRACTICING CHURCH DISCIPLINE

Now let's address two very important questions about the practice of church discipline today. First, why do we practice church discipline? Mark Dever provides five reasons:

1. For the good of the person disciplined
2. For the good of other Christians, as they see the danger of sin
3. For the health of the church as a whole
4. For the corporate witness of the church
5. For the glory of God, as we reflect His holiness[18]

Second, how do we begin to implement church discipline?

1. We must teach our church members what the Bible says about church discipline.
2. We must begin to implement church discipline biblically, lovingly, wisely, gently, and slowly. A cram course and premature action are a certain formula for disaster. If the congregation has not been instructed and prepared, the church could split, or the pastor could be terminated.
3. We must apply church discipline to specific sins like those listed in 1 Corinthians 5:11: sexual immorality, greed, idolatry, reviling, drunkenness, and swindling. We believe this list is selective and not exhaustive. In the modern church issues such as divisiveness, lying, slander, gossip, unrepentance, malice, and absentee membership may also need to be addressed.
4. We must engage in church discipline not to cause hurt but to bring about healing and health in the body of Christ. Bryan Chapell is correct when he writes,

> *"I am writing you not to associate with anyone who bears the name of brother who is sexually immoral or greedy, an idolater or a reviler, a drunkard or a swindler. Do not even eat with such a person."*
>
> **1 Corinthians 5:11**

> There is a difference between needing to divide and loving to divide. A divisive person loves to fight. The differences are usually observable. A person who loves the peace and purity of the church may be forced into division, but it is not his character. He enters arguments regrettably and infrequently. When forced to argue, he remains fair, truthful, and loving in his responses. He grieves to have to disagree with a brother. Those who are divisive by nature lust for the fray, incite its onset, and delight in being able to conquer another person. For them victory means everything. So in an argument they

twist words, call names, threaten, manipulate procedures, and attempt to extend the debate as long as possible and along as many fronts as possible.

Divisive persons frequent the debates of the church. As a result the same voices and personalities tend to appear over and over again, even though the issues change.[19]

Assume that your church has a very large absentee membership. These absentee members fall into four categories:
1. Some live in the church area but attend services only two or three times a year.
2. Some live in the church area but never attend services.
3. Some live a great distance from the church and never attend the services but regularly send financial contributions to the church.
4. Some live a great distance from the church, never attend the services, and never support the church financially.

Your church has asked you to recommend what to do about the absentee members. Think through the situation and state your recommendations.

_____

_____

_____

In the final analysis church discipline is a painful but necessary extension of Christian discipleship. We do it not because it is pleasant but because we must. Why?

Overlooking sin is not gracious but dangerous.

1. Overlooking sin is not gracious but dangerous.
2. Confronting sin is not optional but essential.
3. Dealing with sin is not judgmental but remedial.
4. Correcting sin is not carnal but spiritual.

Thomas Oden says, "Only those who take sin seriously take forgiveness seriously."[20] Our Lord did both, and so must we, as we lovingly and faithfully follow the divine directions for church discipline.

**What would you recommend to your church in each
of the following cases?**

1. A church-elected song leader in a rural church works with a fellow church member in a large warehouse where many unbelievers work. The man constantly takes God's name in vain while on the job. The fellow church member talks with the man in private and asks him not to take God's name in vain. The man tells him to mind his own business and that he will talk any way he wishes.

2. The pastor of a large church is addicted to viewing pornography on his home computer. The church discovers this habit. Confronted by three godly men from the church, the pastor confesses his sin, repents, asks God's forgiveness, and asks the church to forgive him.

3. An adult men's Sunday School teacher begins teaching a hodgepodge of his own ideas that are obviously heretical and not scriptural.

4. A prominent member of the church, a deacon and one of the largest financial contributors, is arrested for driving under the influence of alcohol. His name appears in the local newspaper.

5. A new Christian, a man from a low socioeconomic background, is caught in the clutches of alcoholism and is arrested for DUI. His name appears in the local newspaper.

_____

_____

CAN CHURCH DISCIPLINE REALLY TAKE PLACE TODAY?

Mark and Jim had become so involved in their study that they failed to see it had taken an hour longer than they had planned. The hour was late, but both men knew that their wife and fiancée would not mind. Indeed, both women were excited about what was taking place in the lives of these men.

Mark brought the study to an end by saying, "I have learned a lot about church discipline, and I have come to a conclusion about how my church should address the issue," he said.

"What's that?" Jim asked.

"First," Mark responded, "we can't ignore the issue of church discipline. To do so would ignore clear biblical teachings. But second, my church needs a long process of teaching and guidance before most church members would move in this direction. If we began church discipline tomorrow, I think it would tear the church apart."

"The greatest lesson I learned is that church discipline must be done from love," Jim said. "Most churches don't do church discipline, and some of the few that do seem to do so from a harsh, legalistic spirit. The church is like a family. And true biblical discipline is the result of a healthy family in which there is a lot of love."

"True biblical discipline is the result of a healthy family in which there is a lot of love."

As the men headed to their cars, Jim asked, "What's next week?"

Mark answered, "There has been a lot of talk for several years about the purposes of the church. I think we can tackle that topic next."

"Sounds good," Jim said as he got into his car. And in the car he began thinking, *I really shouldn't have dropped out of church. I see now that the local church, even with all of its flaws and problems, is where I'm supposed to be.* He knew his fiancée would be happy to hear that.

State what you consider to be some key guidelines for a church to follow in implementing church discipline.

State one new thing you learned while studying this chapter.

🔍 Review your memory verses for this chapter.

🔍 Close your study of this chapter by praying the words of Ephesians 5:25-27: "Dear God, I thank you that 'Christ loved the church and gave Himself for her, to make her holy, cleansing her in the washing of water by the word. He did this to present the church to Himself in splendor, without spot or wrinkle or any such thing, but holy and blameless.' Please help our church to be clean and healthy. Guide our church in the area of church discipline. In Jesus' name. Amen."

LEADER GUIDE

DOES MY CHURCH HAVE TO PRACTICE CHURCH DISCIPLINE?

BEFORE THE SESSION

1. Study chapter 4 and complete the learning activities.
2. Obtain a copy of your church's covenant, constitution, and by-laws. Examine them to determine whether anything is stated about church discipline.
3. Write the following Scripture references and instructions on separate index cards.
   - Group 1: *Read Titus 1:10-14. Answer the questions in the activity on pages 96–97.*
   - Group 2: *Read Titus 3:9-11. What did Paul tell Titus to avoid? Why did he tell Titus to avoid these things? How should a divisive person be handled? What is the true condition of a perverted person?*
   - Group 3: *Read Titus 3:9-11. Explain how this passage applies to the local church today.*
   - Group 4: *Read Titus 3:9-11. Rewrite the passage in your own words.*
   - Group 5: *Read 1 Corinthians 5. Complete the activity on page 100.*

DURING THE SESSION

1. Introduce the title of chapter 4. Ask a volunteer to lead in prayer.
2. If your church covenant, constitution, or by-laws make any references to church discipline, read those portions to the group. Ask: *Do we practice these statements? If not, why do you think we fail to do so?*
3. Ask members to identify their feelings and concerns about the practice of church discipline. Write these on a dry-erase board for later reference.
4. Ask members to turn to the activity on page 93. Ask volunteers to read the Scripture passages. As each one is read, ask the group to select the statement to which it refers.
5. Ask: *Why do you think Baptists have neglected church discipline in recent years?* Allow time for discussion. Summarize the discussion by sharing the four reasons on pages 94–95.

6. Divide members into five small groups and give each group an index card with a Scripture reference and instructions. Allow time for group work and call for reports. Allow discussion as reports are shared.

7. Ask: *Why should we practice church discipline?* After responses, summarize:
   - *For the good of the person disciplined*
   - *For the good of other Christians, as they see the danger of sin*
   - *For the health of the church as a whole*
   - *For the corporate witness of the church*
   - *For the glory of God, as we reflect His holiness*

8. Ask the group to study the activity on pages 106. Ask: *What would you recommend about these absentee members?*

9. Divide members into five groups again. Assign each group one of the scenarios in the activity on pages 107–8. Ask each group to discuss the situation and bring recommendations on how the church should handle the problem. Allow time for group work and call for reports.

10. Ask: *What is the role of prayer in church discipline? What is the role of church leaders in church discipline? What is the role of church members in church discipline? What is the role of the Holy Spirit in church discipline?*

11. Refer on the dry-erase board to the list of members' concerns about church discipline. Ask volunteers to summarize how this chapter has addressed each concern.

12. As a group, read aloud the memory verses for chapter 4.

13. Lead the group to read in unison the prayer on page 109.

Chapter 5

HOW DOES A VIBRANT CHURCH CARRY OUT ITS MAIN PURPOSES?

Learning Goals

A study of this chapter will help you gain a better understanding of the primary mission and purposes of the church. You will be motivated to pray more and do more to help your church achieve its mission.

Memory Verses

"All authority has been given to Me in heaven and on earth. Go, therefore, and make disciples of all nations, baptizing them in the name of the Father and of the Son and of the Holy Spirit, teaching them to observe everything I have commanded you. And remember, I am with you always, to the end of the age" (Matt. 28:18-20).

"I assumed," Mark said to Jim, "that most church members know why their churches exist and that we all agree on why the church exists. From our study so far, I'm convinced that is not the case. And I'm not so sure I fully understand what the purposes of a church are."

Jim smiled and responded, "Well, if you don't know what the church is supposed to do, I can assure you that I don't have a clue. I've been out of church too long to know the purposes of the church." And so Mark and Jim began their next study session to more clearly see God's picture for His church.

A BIBLICAL VISION FOR THE CHURCH

Imagine that you started a church from scratch. How would you begin? Where would you look for a blueprint? What would be your mission? Your primary purpose? Your objectives?

State what you consider to be the main mission or purpose of the church.

Now state two or three of the primary ways the church achieves its mission. Later in the study, we will evaluate what you have written.

Mark Dever says, "The proper ends for a local congregation's life and actions are the worship of God, the edification of the church, and the evangelization of the world. These three purposes in turn serve the glory of God."[1] In this chapter we will examine Acts 2:14-47, which reveals the primary mission and purposes of the church. From this passage we will identify essential patterns and practices that constitute a biblical vision for the church today.

The 21st-century church, particularly in America, is suffering an identity crisis. It is not sure who it is or what it should do. It is uncertain how to measure its health and recognize its success. Some say the church must be seeker-sensitive, purpose-driven, relevant, positive, and attractive. Others challenge the church to return to the ancient model in form and practice. Others call the church to doctrinal purity grounded in Reformation theology. And still others call the church to community and authenticity, to experience intimacy and family.

As we carefully, fairly, and honestly evaluate and critique these positions, we find an element of truth in each. Every perspective shares something we need to hear and challenges us to consider issues we dare not ignore.

Explain this statement in your own words: "The 21st-century church, particularly in America, is suffering an identity crisis."

What evidence of this identity crisis have you observed?

How do we keep our equilibrium in the midst of these swirling influences? Even more crucial, what is our source of authority for determining what the church is and does? We believe the answer to both questions is the same. We need a rigorous and clear first-century vision for the 21st-century church. We must take off our cultural blinders, rid ourselves of our personal and theological pet peeves, and work our way to the bedrock basics of Scripture. Here we will catch a vision of the church as God intends it to be.

An excellent place to begin our search is the day the church was born in Acts 2. Here we find a church that pleased and honored God. Five essential features of this first-century church can effectively guide and direct the 21st-century churches of the Lord Jesus Christ.

We need a rigorous and clear first-century vision for the 21st-century church.

List three or four primary characteristics of your church.

_____

_____

How do you think persons outside your church would describe it?

_____

Purposes of the church:
- **Exalt the Savior.**
- **Exposit the Scriptures.**
- **Edify the saints.**
- **Embrace the Spirit.**
- **Evangelize sinners.**

EXALT THE SAVIOR (ACTS 2:22-36)

The context of this passage is the Day of Pentecost and Peter's great Pentecostal sermon. Jesus had ascended in exaltation, and the Holy Spirit had descended as the fulfillment of Old Testament prophecy (see Joel 2) and of Jesus' promise (see John 14–16). The people were confused as the 120 followers of Christ began to speak in languages they were not trained to speak. Erroneously, they concluded that the disciples were drunk. However, no observant Jew would have drunk wine or eaten food before that time on a holy day like Pentecost.

Exalt: glorify, lift up

> Less than two months earlier Peter had denied Jesus. The disciples had deserted Jesus and had been afraid. Now on the Day of Pentecost they were all very bold and began openly witnessing. The change in their lives was due to (check one)—
> ○ 1. the Holy Spirit's coming and taking control of their lives;
> ○ 2. the great gathering in Jerusalem for the festival of Pentecost;
> ○ 3. their knowledge of Old Testament Scripture.

Answer: 1

Peter started where they were, with their confusion and their questions, and immediately focused on Jesus. In verses 22-36, the heart of his message, he made several foundational observations about the person and work of Jesus that are the heart and soul of a gospel witness anyplace and anytime. Curtis Vaughn notes that he begins "with the *man* Jesus" (v. 22) and closes "with the ascended *Lord* (v. 34)."[2]

Read Peter's sermon in Acts 2:22-36. Write the correct verse number(s) beside each statement.

_____ 1. The miracles Jesus did showed that He was sent from God.

_____ 2. The people were aware that Jesus performed miracles.

_____ 3. God planned for Jesus to die on the cross.

_____ 4. Sinful people nailed Jesus to the cross and killed Him.

_____ 5. Both divine sovereignty and human responsibility were involved in Jesus' death.

_____ 6. God raised Jesus from death.

_____ 7. David foresaw the resurrection.

_____ 8. The disciples witnessed the resurrection.

_____ 9. Jesus was exalted to the right hand of God.

_____ 10. Jesus bestowed the Holy Spirit on the disciples.

_____ 11. Jesus is Savior and Lord.

"Men of Israel, listen to these words: This Jesus the Nazarene was a man pointed out to you by God with miracles, wonders, and signs that God did among you through Him, just as you yourselves know."

Acts 2:22

Jesus' accreditation (v. 22). In verse 22 the word *attested* (NASB) means *to vindicate, to approve.* In other words, by the supernatural work of God, it was self-evident who this man was. He was indeed from God. Peter's emphasis on Jesus' accreditation reminds us that the gospel is neither mythology nor fable. It is neither saga nor legend. It is a historical reality grounded in public witness and verifiable testimony.

Read Acts 2:23. Name the two groups of people Peter indicted for Jesus' death.

1. _____   2. _____

"Though He was delivered up according to God's determined plan and foreknowledge, you used lawless people to nail Him to a cross and kill Him."

Acts 2:23

Read Romans 5:6-8 and 1 Corinthians 15:3. Who else is involved in Christ's death on the cross?

_____

Jesus' crucifixion (v. 23). Peter was clear in verse 23: this great One was nailed to a Roman cross and died a shameful and unjust death at the request of the Jewish people. Notice the balance of blame: the Romans were blamed; the Jews were blamed; and if we read the rest of Scripture, we all are to blame. But again notice the balance: God foreordained it, and God purposed it. God's sovereignty was clearly involved. No doubt

Isaiah 53 was running through Peter's mind. Ultimately, Jesus died on the cross because it was the Father's will.

Peter clearly articulated God's sovereignty, and yet he went on to say, "You used lawless people," also affirming human responsibility. In other words, God planned it, and humans are responsible for it. God's sovereignty and human freedom were both involved. John Polhill puts it in perspective: "This double dimension of divine purpose and human responsibility runs throughout Luke-Acts."[3] It should run throughout our theology as well.

Sovereignty: God's supreme rule and authority over the universe

Match each statement with the correct term.

___ 1. "You used lawless people   a. God's sovereignty
to nail Him to a cross
and kill Him" (Acts 2:23).   b. Human freedom
___ 2. "He was delivered up
according to God's
determined plan" (Acts 2:23).

Answers: 1. b, 2. a

Reflect on your conversion experience. How was human freedom involved?

How were God's providence and sovereignty involved?

Jesus' resurrection (vv. 24-32). Verse 24 tells us that God raised Jesus from the dead. Verses 25-28, citing Psalm 16, say that David foresaw the resurrection. Then in verse 29-31 Peter explained it. And in verse 32 the disciples gave evidence that they witnessed it.

Read 1 Corinthians 15:1-8. Complete the following sentences.

1. Jesus died for _____.

2. He was _____.

3. On the third day Jesus was _____.

4. Jesus' death and resurrection were according to _____.

"Since He has been exalted to the right hand of God and has received from the Father the promised Holy Spirit, He has poured out what you both see and hear. For it was not David who ascended into the heavens, but he himself says: The Lord said to my Lord, 'Sit at My right hand until I make Your enemies Your footstool.' Therefore let all the house of Israel know with certainty that God has made this Jesus, whom you crucified, both Lord and Messiah!"

Acts 2:33-36

From the very beginning, Jesus' death and resurrection constituted the core of the Christian gospel and the heart of the church. As far back as you wish to explore Christian history, you find at the very center of the Christian movement the death, burial, and resurrection of Jesus Christ. When we come together as a body of believers, we cannot be an authentic Christian church if the gospel is not front and center in everything we do. That's the problem with some in the seeker-targeted movement. They start in the wrong place. When you start in the wrong place, you end up in the wrong place. In other words, if you start with people—their needs, their feelings, and their wants—you end up with a human-centered church. But if you start with God and the gospel, you speak to the real needs of the human heart. Not only will you begin in the right place, but you will also end up in the right place—with a church that exalts Jesus Christ. The crucifixion and resurrection are at the heart of the gospel message and at the heart of an authentic New Testament church.

Jesus' exaltation (vv. 33-36). Resurrection led to ascension and exaltation. Citing David's realization of this in Psalm 110:1, Peter said it was a signed, sealed, and settled reality that this Jesus whom they crucified was Lord and Christ.

Peter's sermon shows that the first-century church was a Christ-centered church. The believers loved Him, talked about Him, worshiped Him, and shared Him. Adrian Rogers said, "Do not sing songs that a Unitarian can sing. Do not preach sermons a socialist can affirm. Preach the gospel; preach Jesus; make sure you always exalt the Savior." And so the first essential purpose of an authentic church is to be Christ-centered and exalt our Savior.

What are some ways your church exalts the Savior?

_____

_____

What are some ways you personally exalt the Savior?

_____

_____

EXPOSIT THE SCRIPTURES (ACTS 2:17-21,25-28,33-36)

The first-century church was also a Scripture-saturated church. Just as the Word of God was taught on the Day of Pentecost, it was also taught in the days following Pentecost (see v. 42). In his sermon Peter exposited Joel 2; Psalm 16; and Psalm 110. Peter explained these texts in an expositional manner, then gave application to those who heard. Peter understood that apart from the exposition of Scripture, the people would remain confused and unconverted. We know God is sovereign. We know God can do whatever He wishes to do that is consistent with His character, but He has made it clear that He does not convert apart from His Word (see Rom. 10:12-15; 1 Pet. 1:23).

Copies of Scripture were not readily available in New Testament times. The fact that Peter quoted and applied Old Testament passages indicates that (choose the best response)—

○ 1. he had studied the Old Testament Scriptures;

○ 2. Jesus taught Peter and the other disciples the Old Testament Scriptures;

○ 3. the Holy Spirit illumined Peter's mind and helped him remember Scripture;

○ 4. all of the above.

Exposit: explain

"You have been born again—not of perishable seed but of imperishable—through the living and enduring word of God."

1 Peter 1:23

Answer: 4

Read Romans 10:12-15. Match each verse with the correct summary statement(s). More than one statement may apply to some of the verses.

___ 1. Verse 12

___ 2. Verse 13

___ 3. Verse 14

___ 4. Verse 15

a. The gospel is good news.

b. God sends preachers to tell people about Jesus.

c. God has no favorites.

d. A person must believe in Jesus to call on Him.

e. A person must hear about Jesus before she can call on Him.

f. The person who calls on the Lord will be saved.

g. God is merciful to everyone who calls on Him.

Answers: 1. c, g, 2. f, 3. d, e, 4. a, b

You will never build a great church without the Bible as the foundation.

A wise man said, "We are not smart enough to teach anything other than the Bible. And we are too smart to teach anything but the Bible." You can build a large crowd without the Bible as the foundation, but you will never build a great church without the Bible as the foundation. About preaching we must remember, "If preachers preach their own word, the congregation may listen politely but has every right to disregard the sermon as just another person's opinion. If contemporary preachers preach with authority, however, the congregation can no longer dismiss their sermons as merely personal opinions but must respond to them as authoritative messages. … Accordingly, if preachers wish to preach with divine authority, they must proclaim the message of the inspired Scriptures, for the Scriptures alone are the word of God written; the Scriptures alone have divine authority."[4]

Martin Luther, who wrote more than 60,000 pages in his lifetime, said at the end of his life, "I hope all my books would disappear, and the Holy Scriptures alone be read." A vibrant church must expound the Scriptures.

EDIFY THE SAINTS (ACTS 2:42-47)

Jesus commanded his church to be a disciple-making church, a church that is creating little "Christs"—persons who, by the grace of God, are daily being conformed more and more to the image of Jesus. To edify the saints, we must focus on five essentials found in verses 42-47.

A teaching church (v. 42). John Albert Bengel said, "Scripture is the foundation of the Church: the Church is the guardian of Scripture. When the Church is in strong health, the light of Scripture shines bright; when the Church is sick, Scripture is corroded by neglect; and thus it happens, that the outward form of Scripture and that of the Church, usually seem to exhibit simultaneously either health or else sickness; and as a rule the way in which Scripture is being treated is in exact correspondence with the condition of the Church."[5] The church must be consistent in its teaching of biblical doctrine.

John Stott said on this point,

> One might perhaps say that the Holy Spirit opened a school in Jerusalem that day; its teachers were the apostles whom Jesus had appointed; and there were 3,000 pupils in their kindergarten! We note that those new converts were not enjoying a mystical experience which led them to despise their mind or disdain theology. Anti-intellectualism and the fullness of the Spirit are mutually incompatible, because the Holy Spirit is the Spirit of truth. Nor did these early disciples imagine that, because they had received the Spirit, he was the only teacher they needed and they could dispense with human teachers. On the contrary, they sat at the apostles' feet, hungry to receive instruction, and they persevered in it.[6]

Review the previous paragraph and explain in your own words this statement: "Anti-intellectualism and the fullness of the Spirit are mutually incompatible."

Edify: build up

"They devoted themselves to the apostles' teaching."

Acts 2:42

Essentials for edifying the saints:
- **A teaching church**
- **A loving church**
- **A praying church**
- **A giving church**
- **A worshiping church**

George Barna would add, "The church is designed to be a teaching center. However, Christians don't act like Christians because they don't think like Christians. And Christians don't think like Christians because they don't understand their faith."[7] A great church will be a Bible-teaching church.

What are some ways your church teaches and explains God's Word to people?

_____

_____

_____

How do you study the Bible at home? _____

_____

_____

"They devoted themselves to the apostles' teaching, to fellowship, to the breaking of bread, and to prayers. Then fear came over everyone, and many wonders and signs were being performed through the apostles."

Acts 2:42-43

A loving church (v. 42). We must also build and develop a church devoted to fellowship. This community component of a healthy church is expressed in the desire and God-given longing for authentic relationships. Through fellowship we demonstrate the reality of the gospel, the truth of the gospel. All of us need to be reminded of Jesus' words: "By this all people will know that you are My disciples, if you have love for one another" (John 13:35).

Read Acts 2:42. List four things to which the early church was devoted.

1. _____   2. _____

3. _____   4. _____

A praying church (vv. 42-43). The early church was also devoted to prayer. It has been well said that "we move forward with the work of God on our knees." It was this way in the past, and it will certainly be this way

in the future. A prayerless church is a powerless church. Corporate and private prayer is vital to the health and welfare of the body of Christ.

Name some ways your church engages in corporate prayer.

_____

_____

A giving church (vv. 44-45). The word *every* and the word *all* (the same word in the Greek text) occur four times in verses 43-45. Here a genuine community is made evident to all.

Many local churches are hard, harsh, and unloving. Because they are inauthentic in the way they live among themselves, they have little impact on the culture and in their community. In contrast, authentic New Testament churches are a people who look for needs, step up, and meet them. Any Christian or church that sees a genuine need, has the resources to meet that need, but doesn't take action sins against God and His body.

Read Acts 2:44-45 in the margin. These verses teach that (check one)—

○ 1. Christians should help people in need;
○ 2. Christians should practice common ownership of possessions;
○ 3. Christians should not own property.

A worshiping church (vv. 46-47). These verses show both formal and informal worship side by side. Both structured and spontaneous worship are wedded as perfect partners. Adrian Rogers said, "This church was not rusted together by traditionalism. They were not wired together by organization. Nor were they frozen together by formalism. They were melted and brought together by prayer, praise, and the power of the Holy Spirit of God."

I (Danny) heard Alistair Begg say, "Although worship services ought to be dignified, it is not right for worship services to be dull. The Lord Jesus was present. There was reverence and rejoicing. Formality and informality. Structure and absence of structure. Trumpets sounded, cymbals clanged, and other instruments joined in this great cacophony of sound, and they raised their voices in praise to the Lord." There is room for

"All the believers were together and had everything in common. So they sold their possessions and property and distributed the proceeds to all, as anyone had a need."

Acts 2:44-45

"Every day they devoted themselves to meeting together in the temple complex, and broke bread from house to house. They ate their food with gladness and simplicity of heart, praising God and having favor with all the people. And every day the Lord added to them those who were being saved."

Acts 2:46-47

Answer: 1

many varieties and expressions in worship as long as they are grounded in Scripture. Expressions of worship must not detract or distract from the message. If they do, they are out of bounds.

Mark the following statements *T* (true) or *F* (false).

___ 1. Formal worship should be avoided.

___ 2. Worship should always be spontaneous.

___ 3. Worship should not be structured.

___ 4. There are many varieties and expressions of worship.

___ 5. Worship should not be loud.

___ 6. Worship should be grounded in Scripture.

True: 4, 6

False: 1, 2, 3, 5

Like the earliest New Testament church, churches today edify the saints when they are diligent to teach, love, pray, give, and worship.

"Since He has been exalted to the right hand of God and has received from the Father the promised Holy Spirit, He has poured out what you both see and hear."

Acts 2:33

EMBRACE THE SPIRIT (ACTS 2:14-21,33,38)

In verse 33 we see that the Spirit is a gift from the Lord Jesus, and in verse 38 we see that He is crucial to conversion. The Holy Spirit has rightly been described as the misplaced and forgotten member of the Trinity. Because of Pentecostal and charismatic excesses, some churches have overcompensated by negating and neglecting the ministry of the Spirit altogether. But extremism in either direction seriously impairs the health and effectiveness of the church. Again, biblical balance is the essential key.

" 'Repent,' Peter said to them, 'and be baptized, each of you, in the name of Jesus the Messiah for the forgiveness of your sins, and you will receive the gift of the Holy Spirit.' "

Acts 2:38

What are some charismatic excesses in some churches regarding the Holy Spirit?

_____

_____

What are some ways other churches neglect the Holy Spirit?

_____

_____

We should welcome the Spirit as a promise. That is the theme of verses 14-21,33. Peter quoted the prophet Joel's predictions of the great and awesome day that would inaugurate the messianic era and the last days: "I will pour out My Spirit on all humanity. … I will even pour out My Spirit … in those days" (Acts 2:17-18).

> **Believers receive the Holy Spirit (check the correct response)—**
> ○ as a gift from God;
> ○ through works of service.

We should rejoice that the Holy Spirit has manifested Himself in a fresh way through His coming at Pentecost. But we should also welcome the Spirit as a gift. He comes as a promise, but we also receive Him as a gift. In other words, we receive Him by grace as a precious, wonderful gift from God. We do not receive Him through works. We do not receive Him as an obligation. We do not earn Him. We receive Him. In this day He is both with us and in us, and He will be with us forever. Using the Scriptures as our guide, the church needs to regain a healthy interest in and understanding of the role and ministry of the Holy Spirit if it is to be the people of God who move out in His anointing and power.

EVANGELIZE SINNERS (ACTS 2:37-41,47)

A vibrant church exalts Christ, expounds the Scriptures, edifies the saints, and embraces the Spirit. Finally, an authentic church has the goal of evangelizing sinners. A Christ-centered church is a soul-winning church. We must speak to sinners about the Savior.

In verse 37 Peter cut the crowd to their hearts with his preaching. In verse 38 he presented them with four essential components of the salvation experience:

1. Repentance
2. Baptism in the name of Jesus
3. Forgiveness of sins
4. Receiving the Holy Spirit

> **Mark the following statements** *T* **(true) or** *F* **(false).**
> ___ 1. Baptism is essential for salvation.
> ___ 2. Baptism is essential for obedience.

"When they heard this, they were pierced to the heart and said to Peter and the rest of the apostles: 'Brothers, what must we do?' 'Repent,' Peter said to them, 'and be baptized, each of you, in the name of Jesus the Messiah for the forgiveness of your sins, and you will receive the gift of the Holy Spirit.' "

Acts 2:37-38

True: 2

False: 1

Write in your own words the way someone becomes a Christian.

Do not misunderstand us. Baptism is not essential for salvation. However, it is certainly important. The New Testament has no conception of an unbaptized believer, as we noted earlier. Baptism is central to a believer's identification with Christ and His body.

Baptism is central to a believer's identification with Christ and His body.

Southern Baptists are known for being very evangelistic. We baptize about 350,000 people a year, but more than one-third are rebaptisms of adults who were dunked as children. Now as adults, they are convinced that their baptism as a child was inauthentic. That is a scandal we need to address. Baptism requires an understanding of what is taking place when we are saved. Essential for salvation? No. Essential for obedience? Absolutely.

Describe the occasion when you trusted Christ as Savior.

Who helped you make your decision to follow Him?

What do you remember about your baptism?

Who baptized you? _____

Where? _____

Then Peter exhorted them in verse 40: "With many other words he testified and strongly urged them, saying, 'Be saved from this corrupt generation!' " When we speak to sinners about the Savior, as God has promised in His Word, we will see sinners come to the Savior.

We did the math and found something very interesting: the body of Christ multiplied 26 times in one day at Pentecost—from 120 to 3,120. And verse 47 makes it clear that it did not stop there. Unfortunately, many of us are blessed if we see one person a month come to Christ. Some churches do not see Christ enter the hearts of any new believers in a year. What is the problem? It starts with the pastor. One survey revealed that over the past six months, 54 percent of pastors of declining churches did not share the gospel or develop a relationship with an unchurched person with the intention of sharing their faith one time.[8]

"Every day the Lord added to them those who were being saved."

Acts 2:47

If pastors are not sharing the gospel, what makes them think their people will share the gospel? The church's spiritual maturity will never rise any higher than that of its leadership. Church members will not love the Word and prayer more than the leaders do. And they will not love lost souls more than their leaders do.

Summarizing what we find in Acts 2, John Polhill notes that these verses

> give an ideal portrait of the young Christian community, witnessing the Spirit's presence in the miracles of the apostles, sharing their possessions with the needy among them, sharing their witness in the temple, sharing themselves in the intimacy of their table fellowship. Their common life was marked by praise of God, joy in the faith, and sincerity of heart. And in all this they experienced the favor of the non-believers and continual blessings of God-given growth. It was an ideal, almost blissful time marked by the joy of their life together and the warmth of the Spirit's presence among them. … Luke's summaries present an ideal for the Christian community which it must always strive for, constantly return to, and discover anew, if it is to have that unity of Spirit and purpose essential for an effective witness.[9]

Warren Wiersbe notes, "The Christians you meet in the book of Acts were not content to meet once a week for service as usual. They met daily (2:46), cared daily (6:1), won souls daily (2:47), searched the Scriptures daily (17:11), and increased in numbers daily (16:5). Their Christian faith was a day-to-day reality, not a once-a-week routine. Why? Because the risen Christ was a living reality to them, and his resurrection power was at work in their lives through the Spirit."[10]

How do we do church in the 21st century? The answer is easy. We go back and immerse ourselves in the purposes and practices of the first-century church. We go back to the future.

Review the main mission or purpose of the church that you wrote on page 113. How would you revise your statement in light of your study of this chapter?

Review what you wrote on page 113 about the primary ways the church can achieve its mission. How would you revise the statements in light of your study?

Think about your church in light of the five essentials for building up believers: teaching, loving, praying, giving, and worshiping. Evaluate how well you think your church is doing in each area by writing that word at the appropriate place on the following scale.

Improvement needed   Good   Outstanding

How do you think your church is doing in evangelism?

Improvement needed   Good   Outstanding

WHERE DO WE GO FROM HERE?

"We have spent over a month studying the church," Jim sighed.

Mark answered, "And to think it all began because I invited you to my church. I hoped to get you back into church, but now I think God used our study to help me better understand the purposes of the church and what I am supposed to do in the church."

After a brief silence Jim spoke. "OK, Mark, where do we go from here? This study has convinced me that I need to get back in church, but I'm not sure where I'm supposed to go or what I'm supposed to do. What's next?"

Mark spoke carefully. "Jim, will you join me for one more week? I'd like for us to end our study with a look at the big picture of a vibrant church. In the process I think we can come up with some answers to your question."

"I guess one more week won't hurt," Jim laughed.

"Just be patient," Mark said with a smile. "I think your wait will be rewarded."

🔍 **Review your memory verses for this chapter. Ask God to make them a part of your life.**

What do you think God wants you to do in response to your study of this chapter? Write your thoughts here.

🔍 **Pray, asking God to help your church truly reflect the essential purposes of the early church. Ask Him to help you do your part to help make your church what He wants it to be.**

LEADER GUIDE

Session 5

HOW DOES A VIBRANT CHURCH CARRY OUT ITS MAIN PURPOSES?

BEFORE THE SESSION

1. Study chapter 5 and complete the learning activities.
2. Write the following Scripture references and instructions on separate index cards.
   - Group 1: *Read Acts 2:14-36. How did Peter explain what was taking place that day? What did he say about Jesus' life and works? What did he say about Jesus' death and resurrection? What did he say about Jesus' exaltation?*
   - Group 2: *Read Acts 2:37-41. What were the results of Peter's sermon?*
   - Group 3: *Read 1 Corinthians 15:1-8. Identify the basic facts of the gospel as recorded in this passage.*
   - Group 4: *Read Romans 10:8-15. Identify the basic facts of the gospel as recorded in this passage.*
   - Group 5: *Read Acts 2:41-47. What were the activities of the early church?*

DURING THE SESSION

1. Begin with prayer. Announce that the session will focus on events in a day when three thousand persons were saved and baptized. Ask members to describe the occasion when they trusted Christ as Savior. Ask: *Who influenced you to make the decision to follow Jesus? What do you remember about your baptism? Who baptized you? Where?*
2. Ask: *What do you consider the main mission or purpose of the church? Allow time for sharing.* Then ask: *What are some of the primary ways the church achieves its mission?* Allow time for sharing.
3. Ask members to turn to Acts 2 in their Bibles. Summarize Acts 2:1-13.
4. Divide into five small groups and give each group a card with a Scripture reference and instructions. Allow time for group work and call for reports. Permit discussion and questions as the reports are shared.
5. Ask: *What are the main features or activities that define our church? Allow time for sharing.* Then ask: *How do you think persons outside our church would describe us?*

6. State that Acts 2:22-47 identifies five features of the early church. Write on a dry-erase board: *Exalt the Savior, Exposit the Scriptures, Edify the Saints, Embrace the Spirit, Evangelize Sinners.* Ask members to gather in the same five groups as before. Assign one function to each of the five groups. Ask each group to use the material in chapter 5 (pp. 115–28) to define each function and to identify ways your church carries out these functions. After group work, call for reports.

7. Read Acts 2:42-47 and identify five ways the early church edified the saints: teaching, loving, praying, giving, worshiping. Write these on a dry-erase board. Point out that these activities should be prominent parts of church life today. Ask: *What are some ways our church teaches God's Word? Is our church known for its fellowship and love? What are some ways our church engages in corporate prayer? What are some ways our church tries to meet others' needs?*

8. Ask members to describe their church's worship style and practices. Ask for responses to the true/false activity on page 124. Allow time for discussion.

9. Instruct members to respond to the evaluations on pages 128–29. Ask them to identify ways their church can improve in areas of weakness.

10. Ask the group to read aloud together the memory verses for chapter 5.

11. Close by praying that God will help your church faithfully carry out the purposes of a New Testament church.

12. Ask members to read chapter 6 and to complete the learning activities before the next session.

Chapter 6

WHAT SHOULD A VIBRANT CHURCH LOOK LIKE IN THE 21ST CENTURY?

Learning Goals

A study of this chapter will help you gain a better understanding of what a healthy church should look like. You will be able to evaluate your church in light of the New Testament model.

Memory Verses

"I, therefore, the prisoner in the Lord, urge you to walk worthy of the calling you have received, with all humility and gentleness, with patience, accepting one another in love, diligently keeping the unity of the Spirit with the peace that binds us" (Eph. 4:1-3).

Jim began their conversation, knowing he and Mark were nearing the end of their study: "I think we've learned a lot about the New Testament church, don't you?"

"Yes, I'm both pleased and surprised at how much we have learned about the early church. I can clearly see ways churches today try to follow the New Testament model; yet I can also see how far some have departed from it," Mark responded.

Jim thought for a minute before saying, "So what does all this mean? Early in the study you said you were frustrated by the differences between the early church and churches today. You also said the reason I didn't see the church as relevant was because I was probably basing my opinion on weak or nonbiblical churches."

Turning back through his notes, Mark answered, "Remember that intriguing quote from Millard Erickson: '[God] is no longer viewed as relating to the world only through the agency of his supernatural institution, the church, but also dynamically relating to the world through many avenues or institutions. The emphasis is on what God is doing, not on what he is like. Consequently, more attention is given to the mission of the church than to its identity.'[1] That's where we started. Then we looked at definitions of *church* to understand its nature. Then we focused on issues the church is dealing with today."

"If Erickson is correct, then," Jim continued, "where does that leave us with the church today? Is it biblically based? Is it dynamic? What is God doing in the world today, specifically through the church? I guess the bottom line for me is, how can I identify a church that is both biblical and relevant in the world today? How can I know whether a church is one I will want to be a part of?"

"Let's continue our study and see whether we can identify the characteristics of a church that would attract you and other unchurched people—a vibrant church," Mark said as he opened his Bible.

WHAT DOES A VIBRANT CHURCH LOOK LIKE?

We love football! Pop Warner leagues for children, high school, college, or professional—we love it all. We both watched our seven sons (Danny, four; Thom, three) play different sports. Because they went to the same middle and high schools, we sometimes annoyed people with our duet of shouts and encouragement. But it is fascinating and exciting to watch the offensive, defensive, and special teams come together as a coordinated and united fighting machine with one goal in mind: to win the game.

It also amazes us to see how each team member brings his own particular skills and talents to his position and to think how comical and tragic it would be if he brought those same skills and talents to the wrong position. Imagine a quarterback as a nose guard, a guard as a safety, or a tailback as a defensive end! It's not a pretty picture. However, when each one is in just the right position, doing the right job with the goal of team victory before his eyes, the team just might win the national championship or the Super Bowl!

What is true of football is equally true of the body of Christ. When each church member is in the right position, doing the right job for the right reason, your church just might win your community and influence the world for the glory of God and the honor of His Son, Jesus. That's what it means to be a vibrant church.

What does a vibrant church look like? When God puts His team together, what shape will it take? What will your assignment be? What position will you play? In Ephesians 4:1-16 Paul presented four characteristics of a healthy church made up of healthy Christians. This text wonderfully complements what we studied in Acts 2.

A VIBRANT CHURCH IS CHARACTERIZED BY UNITY (EPH. 4:1-6)

Characteristics of a healthy church:
- **Unity**
- **Diversity**
- **Ministry**
- **Maturity**

God desires unity or oneness in the body of Christ. Unity is not uniformity. Uniformity, which takes place when we look alike and act alike, is boring and of limited use. Unity takes place when we walk together and work together with common convictions and commitments. Two such convictions are presented in this text.

Explain in your own words this statement: "Unity is not uniformity."

_____

_____

Write your own definition of *unity*. _____

_____

_____

> **Unity in a vibrant church:**
> • Oneness of humility or behavior
> • Oneness of theology or belief

Oneness of humility or behavior. This is the theme of verses 1-3 and something the early church emphasized. *Therefore* in verse 1 connects chapters 4–6, which emphasize duty, with chapters 1–3, which emphasize doctrine. In other words, belief is the emphasis in chapters 1–3; behavior is the emphasis in chapters 4–6. The order matters. Doctrine always precedes and is the foundation for duty.

Examine the following two statements. Place a check beside the correct statement.
○ 1. Our behavior grows from our belief.
○ 2. Our belief grows from our behavior.

> **Answer: 1**

Someone has said, "We are a lot better at believing than behaving." Check the one that is most difficult for you.
○ Belief ○ Behavior

Read Ephesians 4:1. *Walk* in this verse means—
○ 1. our physical walk;
○ 2. our whole manner of living;
○ 3. our doctrinal beliefs.

Paul, as the Lord's prisoner (not Rome's!), urged or encouraged the Ephesians to "walk worthy of the calling you have received." "Walk" will be a key concept in the remainder of this letter (see 4:17; 5:2,8,15). Kent Hughes notes that to walk worthy is "to live lives equal to the great

> *"I, therefore, the prisoner in the Lord, urge you to walk worthy of the calling you have received."*
>
> Ephesians 4:1

> **Answer: 2**

blessings described in chapters 1 through 3."[2] We are to walk worthy of our calling—"the sovereign, saving calling of God."[3]

Write Ephesians 4:1 in your own words. _____

_____

_____

Read 1 John 2:6. Supply the missing words: "The one who says he remains in Him should walk _____ ."

Now read Genesis 5:24 and supply the missing word: "Enoch _____ with God." For that to be true in your life, what are two changes you need to make?

1. _____

2. _____

Read Ephesians 4:1-3. List five characteristics of our Christian walk.

1. _____   2. _____

3. _____   4. _____

5. _____

> "I, therefore, the prisoner in the Lord, urge you to walk worthy of the calling you have received, with all humility and gentleness, with patience, accepting one another in love, diligently keeping the unity of the Spirit with the peace that binds us."
>
> Ephesians 4:1-3

This calling is both to salvation and to service. It has ethical and moral ramifications that include humility, gentleness, and patience. They involve accepting one another in love, diligently keeping the unity of the Spirit with the peace that binds us. Notice that this unity is kept, not created, by the ministry of the Spirit who binds us together.

Oneness of theology or belief. This is the focus of verses 4-6. Theology really matters. What we believe is wedded to the way we live. The two always go together.

Read Ephesians 4:4-6. State seven aspects of the church's theological unity.

1. _____

2. _____

3. _____

4. _____

5. _____

6. _____

7. _____

[4]"There is one body and one Spirit, just as you were called to one hope at your calling; [5]one Lord, one faith, one baptism, [6]one God and Father of all, who is above all and through all and in all."

Ephesians 4:4-6

Note how Ephesians 4:4-6 refers to the unity of the Trinity.
Verse _____ refers to Jesus.
Verse _____ refers to God the Father.
Verse _____ refers to the Holy Spirit.

Verses 4-6 identify seven facets of our theological unity. These verses also testify to the unity of the three persons of the Trinity. Verse 4 is the Spirit's verse, verse 5 is the Son's verse, and verse 6 is the Father's verse. As our triune God is one, we must be one. Warren Wiersbe notes, "Many people today attempt to unite Christians in a way that is not biblical. ... They will say: 'We are not interested in doctrines, but in love. Now, let's forget our doctrines and just love one another!' " Wiersbe then adds, "While not all Christians agree on some minor matters of Christian doctrine, they all do agree on the foundation truths of the faith. Unity built on anything other than Bible truth is standing on a very shaky foundation."[4]

What are the seven theological essentials that unite a vibrant church?

1. One body. This is the body of Christ of which each believer is a member. "The One Body is the model for the many local bodies that God has established across the world. The fact that a person is a member of the One Body does not excuse him from belonging to a local body; for it is there that he exercises his spiritual gifts and helps others to grow."[5]

Theological essentials that unite a vibrant church:
- **One body**
- **One Spirit**
- **One hope**
- **One Lord**
- **One faith**
- **One baptism**
- **One God and Father**

2. *One Spirit.* This is the Holy Spirit who indwells each believer. As just noted, He binds us to one another in peace.

3. *One hope.* This refers to the "common goal toward which all who belong to the body are progressing … of sharing ultimately in the glory of God."[6] The Holy Spirit within us is the assurance of this great promise (see Eph. 1:13-14).

4. *One Lord.* This is our Lord Jesus Christ who died for us, rose for us, and will one day come for us. As Lord, He is our sovereign Master and King.

5. *One faith.* There is one settled body of truth deposited by Christ for His church. Jude calls it "the faith that was delivered to the saints once for all" (Jude 3). The early Christians recognized a body of basic doctrine that they taught, guarded, and committed to others (see 2 Tim. 2:2).

6. *One baptism.* This is probably the baptism of the Spirit, the act of the Spirit by which He places believers into the body of Christ at conversion (see 1 Cor. 12:13).

7. *One God and Father.* Paul repeatedly emphasized God as Father (see Eph. 1:3,17; 2:18; 3:14; 5:20). We are children in the same family, loving and serving the same Father. Thus, we should walk together in both behavior and belief.

Match the following statements with the related terms.

____ 1. We love and serve the same Father.

____ 2. Jesus died for us, rose for us, and will one day come for us.

____ 3. Each Christian belongs to this.

____ 4. The early Christians recognized a body of basic doctrine.

____ 5. The common goal toward which all believers are progressing

____ 6. The Holy Spirit indwells each believer.

____ 7. The act of the Holy Spirit by which He places believers into the body of Christ at conversion

a. One body
b. One Spirit
c. One hope
d. One Lord
e. One faith
f. One baptism
g. One God and Father

A VIBRANT CHURCH IS CHARACTERIZED BY DIVERSITY (EPH. 4:7-11)

When Jesus returned to heaven, He did not leave His church empty-handed. As the ascended Lord, He poured out spiritual gifts on His body for service to that body. Jesus not only saved us from sin, but He also saved us for service. Each one of us has received enabling grace in the precise and exact proportion Christ gave it to us.

What did Jesus save us from?

What did Jesus save us for?

Citing Psalm 68:18, Paul saw Christ's incarnation and ascension as evidence that God had come and rescued His people as their victorious King. Having received the gifts, the spoils of His victory over sin, death, hell, and the grave (the thrust of Ps. 68:18), our Lord now gives back to His people spiritually gifted men and women to minister to His people, His church. Christ, the ascended Lord, has led captive the powers of evil that attacked, conquered, and enslaved us. The One who came all the way down has now gone all the way up. In so doing, He is far above all, fills all, and gives gifts to all.

Spiritual gifts are mentioned in four texts of Scripture: Romans 12; 1 Corinthians 12; Ephesians 4; and 1 Peter 4. Ephesians 4:7 affirms that every believer has at least one spiritual gift. Spiritual gifts are not natural talents, which are received by natural birth. Spiritual gifts are received by spiritual birth. Often the two have nothing in common.

Stephen Olford often said in his preaching, "God only makes originals, never duplicates." Describe two or three ways you are an original.

"Grace was given to each one of us according to the measure of the Messiah's gift. For it says: When He ascended on high, He took prisoners into captivity; He gave gifts to people. But what does 'He ascended' mean except that He descended to the lower parts of the earth? The One who descended is the same as the One who ascended far above all the heavens, that He might fill all things. And He personally gave some to be apostles, some prophets, some evangelists, some pastors and teachers."

Ephesians 4:7-11

Describe two natural talents God has blessed you with.

1. _____   2. _____

Read Romans 12:6-8 and 1 Corinthians 12:4-11. Describe two spiritual gifts God has given to you.

1. _____   2. _____

Ephesians 4:11 highlights four spiritual gifts that are essential to the health of the church. The phrase "He personally" is emphatic. Christ and no one else gave us these gifted saints.

Apostles and prophets are foundational to the church's mission.

1. Apostles and prophets are foundational to the church's mission. *Apostle*, in a technical sense, refers to the twelve disciples; in a general sense, to anyone who is sent. It can be used to describe missionaries today.
2. Prophets are forth-tellers even more than future-tellers. Prophets are bold proclaimers of God's revelation.
3. Evangelists are "spiritual obstetricians" gifted in bringing forth new births. Some, like Billy Graham, Luis Palau, and Jay Strack, do it before large crowds. Others, like Bobby Welch and Bill Fay, are gifted in sharing their faith one-to-one.
4. "Pastors and teachers" is best translated "pastor-teachers." They are "spiritual pediatricians" who lead and feed, provide for and protect. They minister to us and with us but not for us. Why make this distinction? Because of our next topic.

Match each phrase with the correct term.

____ 1. Can be used to describe missionaries   a. Apostles

____ 2. Those who lead and feed, provide for and protect   b. Prophets

____ 3. Bold proclaimers of God's truth   c. Evangelists

____ 4. Those who are gifted in bringing forth new births   d. Pastors and teachers

Answers: 1. a, 2. d, 3. b, 4. c

A VIBRANT CHURCH IS CHARACTERIZED BY MINISTRY (EPH. 4:12-14)

Read Ephesians 4:12-14. State five things God wills
for every church.

1. Verse 12: _____

2. Verse 12: _____

3. Verse 13: _____

4. Verse 13: _____

5. Verse 14: _____

Check your work as you read. It's all right if you used
different terms from those in the following section.

12"... for the training of the saints in the work of ministry, to build up the body of Christ, 13until we all reach unity in the faith and in the knowledge of God's Son, growing into a mature man with a stature measured by Christ's fullness. 14Then we will no longer be little children, tossed by the waves and blown around by every wind of teaching, by human cunning with cleverness in the techniques of deceit."

Ephesians 4:12-14

"Every member a minister" is a worthy motto for any church. It is also the biblical model. Notice five things God wills for every church's ministry.

Be equipped (Eph. 4:12). The church is not a bus on which the pastor does all the driving and does his best to persuade as many as he can to get on board. The church is a body in which everyone has a function to perform, a part to play. *Equipping* (v. 12, NASB) means *to put in place, to reset dislocated bones, to be made complete*. Why? For the work of the ministry. We all have a work of ministry grounded in the spiritual gifts God gave us. God gifted your pastor to do some things you can't do, but He also gifted you to do some things your pastor can't do.

Name two ways your church equips its members for service.

1. _____

2. _____

Be edified (Eph. 4:12). When all of us do our part, the church, the body of Christ, grows. It grows up (worship). It grows out (evangelism). It grows within (discipleship). It is edified, made strong, vibrant, alive!

God's will for every church's ministry:
- Be equipped.
- Be edified.
- Be educated.
- Be enlarged.
- Be established.

Never confuse movement with action. Just because we are moving does not mean we are going anywhere. We want to go and grow to be the church God saved us to be.

Match each statement with the term that describes that growth.

_____ 1. The church grows out.　　　　a.　Worship

_____ 2. The church grows up.　　　　b.　Evangelism

_____ 3. The church grows within.　　c.　Discipleship

Answers: 1. b, 2. a, 3. c

Be educated (Eph. 4:13). God has a destiny, a goal at which His church is to aim. It consists of three parts:

1. Unity in the faith
2. Knowledge—full and experiential knowledge of the Son
3. A perfect, complete, mature person

God wants us to know Him and to know Him truthfully.

Be enlarged (Eph. 4:13). The verse reads, "... until we all reach ... a mature man with a stature measured by Christ's fullness." God did not save us simply to take us to heaven. He saved us to make us like Jesus (see Rom. 8:29). That goal will never change, and someday it will be perfectly completed. We must be enlarged after the model of our Savior.

Be established (Eph. 4:14). "Children" in verse 14 refers to a spiritually immature baby or child, in contrast with the mature man in verse 13.

"Those He foreknew He also predestined to be conformed to the image of His Son, so that He would be the firstborn among many brothers."
Romans 8:29

Read Ephesians 4:14. State four ways Paul describes a spiritually immature person.

1. _____

2. _____

3. _____

4. _____

The immature are never settled; they are fickle, shifting, and undependable. They have no roots, no convictions, and no commitments. When tough times come, they run. When a slick presentation is made, they are deceived. Without grounding in biblical doctrine, they are blown about, tricked with loaded dice, fooled by clever schemes, and deceived by the plots of the Evil One.

They are more likely to trust their own reason, experience, and feelings and human advice rather than trust God's counsel. Be established in spiritual truth. Know the Word and obey the Word. What will be the result for the church?

A VIBRANT CHURCH IS CHARACTERIZED BY MATURITY (EPH. 4:15-16)

Members of a vibrant church must be mature in our speech. We continually speak with love *(agape)*, and we grow up in Christ, who is our head, our Lord. We speak the truth, but we do it in love. If we can't say it in love, we need to keep quiet.

We began with love (see Eph. 4:2), and we end with love. When we all do our part, the body grows, and the body is built up in love. What does it look like when an individual member of the body does his or her part to build up the body of Christ?

- It looks like language therapist Lucy Smith and her faith-based literacy program for Texas prisoners. She spends eight hours a day in Dallas and Fort Worth jails. A grandmother of seven, Smith oversees 44 tutors, who teach about 60 inmates a week. Her efforts have caught the attention of state-prison officials, who are now encouraging the development of faith-based programs across the state.
- It looks like 93-year-old Karl Mix, who, after a life of ministry to shut-ins in hospitals, sanitariums, and prisons, volunteered his services at a geriatric-psychiatry center in Canton, Ohio, where he visited patients once a week and led Sunday-morning services.
- It looks like Lieutenant Jeff Francis, who, as the founder of the Chattanooga, Tennessee, police department's first gang division, spends his days working with troubled youth. Then he goes home and works with troubled adults. For the past 16 years he and his wife, Gail, have cared for mentally handicapped adults as house-parents for the Orange Grove Center. They also homeschool their four children and interpret for the deaf in their local church.

"Speaking the truth in love, let us grow in every way into Him who is the head—Christ. From Him the whole body, fitted and knit together by every supporting ligament, promotes the growth of the body for building up itself in love by the proper working of each individual part."

Ephesians 4:15-16

Name two persons in your church who model Ephesians 4:16.
Describe what they do to help the body grow.

1. _____

2. _____

What part do you play in helping your church grow and build
itself up in love?

_____

_____

_____

This is what a healthy churches look like: each member doing his or her
part for the good of others and the glory of God—not just inside the
church walls but also representing the church in the world. God's will is
that we be a vibrant church. To be a vibrant church, we must be vibrant
Christians. Then and only then can we play the part He has for each of
us in the body of Christ.

To be a vibrant church, we must be vibrant Christians.

Assume that your church has asked you to recommend a logo
for the church. The logo will be used on the church sign and
on all church mailings. Consider everything you have studied
about a vibrant church. Recalling the mission and ministry
of your church, draw a sketch of the logo.

Assume that a close non-Christian friend sees your sketch and asks you to explain the logo. Write your explanation below.

_____

_____

_____

A BLUEPRINT FOR CHANGE

At 7:00 p.m. the doorbell rang. When Jim opened the door, he was surprised to see the pastor of Mark's church. Mark introduced Pastor Brad, and the three men went to the kitchen table to talk.

"To what do I owe this honor?" Jim asked.

"Jim," Mark began, "when we began doing this study on the church, I told Brad what we were up to. A couple of weeks later he asked what we were learning, so I began sharing with him about our work. I guess the best way to describe it is that Brad became convinced …"

"Let me interrupt and clarify Jim," Brad said quickly. "I did not just become convinced. I became convicted. In fact, when Mark and I met last week, I began to cry openly. That's not my personality, but I was so convicted about what God wants me to do about my church and my leadership that it broke my heart."

Jim did not speak, so Pastor Brad continued: "I've been a pastor for nearly 20 years. I've had some good days and some bad days; but overall, I'm not satisfied with my church or my leadership.

"When I heard that you and Mark were studying the vibrant church, a church that is really alive and meaningful, I knew I could no longer be satisfied with business as usual. I wanted my church to be a vibrant church."

The humbled pastor continued, "I met with key church leaders this past week, and I plan to share this with the entire church next week. We are going to get serious about church. We will no longer be passive about church membership and commitment."

The pastor then handed some papers to the other two men. "Guys, here are some of my initial thoughts," Brad said. "I'm trying to make practical application of all this good history and Bible study you've given

"We will no longer be passive about church membership and commitment."

me. Tell me what you think. It's just a beginning point, and my leaders like it. But you guys are my human inspiration for these moves, so I really want your input.

Brad then began to outline an initial, five-point plan to move his church toward greater health. He knew it was not final, but it had to begin at a point that the church could handle.

Our church will take membership seriously. "Our tradition has been for a person to walk an aisle and fill out a membership card," Brad began. "We will continue to have a public invitation, but prospective members must attend a four-hour membership class, where we will review *The Baptist Faith and Message*, the purposes and marks of a biblical church, the history of our church and the Southern Baptist Convention, and key biblical doctrines. One of those doctrines will be salvation. I am sad to say that right now I don't know whether even half of our members are Christians. We will no longer take for granted that anyone is saved. We will present the gospel biblically and clearly. I hope this way we can begin moving toward a regenerate church membership.

"We will also begin cleaning our membership roles. I realize I have to be careful doing that because some Baptists seem to equate being on a membership roll with getting a ticket to heaven," Brad laughed. "But we can at least begin to find out whether any of our members are deceased or members of other churches. And if we can't find anything about a member, we will drop that person from our roll."

Our church will become more serious about baptism and the Lord's Supper. "I have never preached a sermon on baptism," Brad confessed. "We take it too lightly in our church. But I will begin a three-part sermon series on baptism, and in the membership class we will teach the significance of baptism.

"The church and I have also been lackadaisical about the Lord's Supper. We tack it on to end of the worship service once a quarter, but we never talk about its significance or meaning. That will change right away."

The pastor's preaching will become more Word-based. "I'm afraid I've been caught in the winds of fads," Brad continued. "I really haven't focused on biblical, expository preaching. It's sad to say, but members have probably learned very little about the Bible from my sermons. They've heard some good stories and illustrations, but those should only supplement my sermons for application. I'm determined to be more

> **"We will no longer take for granted that anyone is saved."**

Word-based in my preaching. I guess I've just been too lazy in that regard. Good biblical preaching demands study—lots of study."

Our church will become more evangelistic and missions-minded. "In the near future," Brad continued, "I will preach through the Book of Acts. I will teach the congregation about the church's missionary responsibility. I will show them the power of Spirit-led evangelism. I will teach them that evangelism and missions are not optional for a vibrant church. I will also look for ways to make evangelism and missions a part of the DNA of our church. We will strive to become more outwardly focused every day."

We will begin to seriously consider church discipline. "I have to admit," Brad said, "that this one scares me a bit. My leaders are behind me, but I have heard horror tales about what happens to churches when they really get serious about church discipline. In fact, I have a pastor friend who was fired over this issue a couple of years ago."

> **"Evangelism and missions are not optional for a vibrant church."**

Mark offered some encouragement. "Look, Brad," he began. "This process will be incremental. You already have buy-in from the leadership. You will begin teaching and preaching about it over time. We will cover church discipline in the membership class. And you will have already made some small steps toward church discipline by cleaning the membership rolls. We are making a statement that we take membership seriously, and that is a huge first step.

"I pray," Mark continued, "that we won't have to face some of those messy church-discipline issues. But if we do, we will be on our knees in prayer. We have no option. It's in the Bible; it's one mark of a New Testament church. No family shows true love unless it is willing to discipline the family members. That goes for the church family as well."

BECOMING A VIBRANT CHURCH

"You know, guys," the pastor said thoughtfully. "I really think there is a good opportunity that we will become that vibrant church you studied. I know these first five steps are only a beginning point, but I'm excited. For the first time in many years, I am excited about being a pastor. And my leaders are excited as well. We all feel that we are about to be a part of something that will really make a difference."

To this point Jim had been very quiet. He and his fiancée had already begun attending Brad and Mark's church, so it wouldn't be accurate to call them unchurched anymore. Still, Jim felt like an outsider eavesdropping on a family conversation. And he was taken aback by Pastor Brad's transparency.

But Jim had some burning questions that had not been answered, so he finally them. "Guys, I'm really confused," he began. "I see how all this makes sense for you and your church. But why are you telling me all this? Why did you come to my house to discuss this?"

Brad and Mark smiled at Jim and each other. Mark spoke first: "Jim, we came here to let you know that we're getting serious about church. And we plan to start our first membership class right after you get married. We are here to ask you and Patti to become founding members of our first class. We think you can give us good advice on how to make it better in the future."

Pastor Brad joined in: "Jim we know you want to be part of a church that's serious about what it does. We want you to be part of that transformation in our church."

Now Jim understood. He was part of something that only God could have orchestrated. In just a few weeks he had moved from unchurched to visiting church, and soon he would be part of a congregation that was trying to take church seriously.

"I guess I'm a bit overwhelmed by all this," Jim said. "I'll have to talk to Patti, but I know she'll be totally on board. She's been waiting for me to make a church decision."

The three men had a time of prayer. As Mark and Brad were leaving, Jim offered some final comments: "This all started rather innocently. Mark and I got involved in a study about the church, and look what happened. It seems that I'm not going to be part of just any church; I will join a church that has decided to become serious about being a church. What did we call it, Mark?"

> **"I will join a church that has decided to become serious about being a church."**

"Vibrant church," Mark responded. "A church that's alive and making a difference."

"That's it," Jim remembered. "Guys, thank you. Thank you for caring about me. And thank you for caring about God's church. I will see you shortly at His next vibrant church."

Read the four statements below that describe a healthy church. Prayerfully and without being critical, evaluate your church in light of each statement. Place the number corresponding to the statement on the scale to indicate the health of your church in that area.

1. A healthy church is characterized by unity.
2. A healthy church is characterized by diversity.
3. A healthy church is characterized by ministry.
4. A healthy church is characterized by maturity.

Attention is needed   Good health   Outstanding health

Review your study of this book and state two or three of the most life-changing things you have learned.

_____

_____

_____

_____

Do you remember Jim's questions at the beginning of the study? Answer them in light of what you have learned in this study. If your answer is yes or no, explain why.

1. Do I really need to belong to a church to be a good Christian?

_____

_____

_____

_____

2. Why can't I practice my faith without attending church?

_____

_____

_____

_____

3. What does the church really do anyway? _____

_____

_____

_____

_____

4. What is the purpose of the church? _____

_____

_____

_____

_____

_____

_____

5. Does the church really matter today?

Review all of your memory verses for the study: 1 Peter 2:9;
Ephesians 4:1-6,11-13; Galatians 6:1-2; Matthew 28:18-20.
Practice them and continue to make them part of your life.

Spend time in prayer, thanking God for your church and
asking Him to help your church be healthy and strong.
Thank Him for the leaders of your church and ask Him
to help them in their ministries. Ask God to equip you
to do your part in helping your church remain healthy.

LEADER GUIDE

Session 6

WHAT SHOULD A VIBRANT CHURCH LOOK LIKE IN THE 21ST CENTURY?

BEFORE THE SESSION

1. Study chapter 6 and complete the learning activities.
2. Write the following Scripture references and instructions on separate index cards:
   - Group 1: *Read Ephesians 4:1-3. How should a Christian conduct his or her daily life? What are five characteristics that should distinguish a believer's walk? What are some ways we can develop these characteristics in our lives?*
   - Group 2: *Read Ephesians 4:1-6. What is the basis of our unity? What are seven aspects of the church's unity?*
   - Group 3: *Read Ephesians 4:7-11. Does each Christian receive spiritual gifts? Who bestows gifts to believers? How do spiritual gifts display diversity in the body of Christ? What are four special gifts Christ gave to the church as a body?*
   - Group 4: *Read Ephesians 4:11-14. What are five things God wills for every church's ministry?*
   - Group 5: *Read Ephesians 4:11-16. What is a Christian's ultimate goal? What is Paul's description of a spiritually immature person? What are two marks of maturity in our speech? What results when every believer does his or her part in the church?*
3. Have available large sheets of paper and felt-tip pens.

DURING THE SESSION

1. Begin with prayer. Share the title of chapter 6 and the learning goal on page 132.
2. Point out this chapter's memory verses, Ephesians 4:1-3, on page 132. Lead the group to read the verses aloud. State that these verses are at the heart of this session.
3. Using the word *therefore* in Ephesians 4:1 and material from the text, explain that Ephesians 1–3 deals with doctrine, or belief, while Ephesians 4–6 deals with duty, or behavior. Emphasize that both are important.
4. Divide members into five groups. Ask each group to study Ephesians 4:1 and to write the verse in its own words. Then call for each group to read its paraphrase. Read Ephesians 4:1 from *The Message:* "*In light of all this, here's what I want you to do. While I'm locked up here, a prisoner for the Master, I want you to get out there and walk—*

better yet, run!—on the road God called you to travel. I don't want any of you sitting around on your hands. I don't want anyone strolling off, down some path that goes nowhere."

5. Give each of the five small groups one of the cards with Scripture references and instructions. As groups work, write these words on a dry-erase board: *Unity, Diversity, Ministry, Maturity.* Allow time for work and call for reports. After group 2 reports, ask members to turn to Ephesians 4:4-6 in their Bibles. Read the statements from the activity on page 138. As each statement is read, ask volunteers to identify the aspect of unity to which it refers. Then continue with the reports.

6. Quote Stephen Olford's words on page 139: *"God only makes originals, never duplicates."* Ask volunteers to read Romans 12:6-8 and 1 Corinthians 12:4-11. Emphasize that each believer is a designer original whom God has gifted to perform a unique ministry.

7. Explain that you will read statements or questions that will help members apply the concepts of unity, diversity, ministry, and maturity. Ask volunteers to complete the following: *How does each of the following help us walk worthy of the calling we have received: God's Word, prayer, fellow believers, and the church? One problem I experience in living a consistent Christian life is … One of the most humble persons I know is … One of the most gentle persons I've ever known is … One of the most patient persons I know is … A problem I have in being patient with others is … One way I have learned to appreciate people different from me is … One thing we can do to promote unity in the church is … A natural talent I have is … A spiritual gift God has given to me is … I use my spiritual gifts by … I receive the most fulfillment in church by my involvement in … One problem I have in exercising my spiritual gifts is … One way other believers have helped me is by … Why are some Christians blown around by every wind of teaching? How can we keep from being blown around by every wind of teaching? What's wrong with speaking the truth without love? What's wrong with speaking in love without truth?* Read Ephesians 4:16.

8. Divide members into five groups. Hand out large sheets of paper and felt-tip pens. Ask each group to suppose your church has asked it to design a logo for use on the church sign and on all church mailings. Ask the groups to reflect on everything they have studied about a healthy church, to consider your church's mission and ministry, and to draw a sketch of their logos. Call for the groups to display their work.

9. Call attention to the learning activity on page 149. Ask members to silently evaluate your church in the areas of unity, diversity, ministry, and maturity.

10. Call attention to the activity on pages 149–51 that lists the questions asked by Jim. Involve members in discussing and responding to the questions.

11. Ask members to share changes their church needs to implement, based on what they have learned in this study. Thank members for participating in the study. Close by asking members to pray in pairs for their church and for their roles in the ministry of their church.

CHAPTER 1

1. Millard Erickson, *Christian Theology*, vol. 3 (Grand Rapids: Baker, 1985), 1038.
2. Discussion by L. Coenen, "Church," in *New International Dictionary of New Testament Theology*, ed. Colin Brown (Grand Rapids: Zondervan, 1975), 1:292–96, as quoted in John Hammett, *Biblical Foundations for Baptist Churches* (Grand Rapids: Kregel, 2005), 27.
3. Robert L. Saucy, *The Church in God's Program* (Chicago: Moody, 1972) 12.
4. Ibid., 16.
5. Ibid., 15.
6. Ibid., 17.
7. Ibid., 18.
8. Ibid., 11.
9. Hammett, 31. This section on biblical images of the church draws significantly from Hammett's excellent analysis, 32–48.
10. Ibid., 36.
11. Ibid., 41.
12. Ibid.
13. Ibid., 43.
14. Ibid., 49.
15. Several excellent resources are available for those who want to examine our history in greater detail. The classic resource work is W. L. Lumpkin, *Baptist Confessions of Faith* (Valley Forge: Judson, 1959; rev. ed. 1969). We also commend the excellent works of Mark Dever, ed., *Polity: A Collection of Historic Baptist Documents* (Center for Church Reform, 2001) and Timothy and Denise George, eds., *Baptist Confessions, Covenants, and Catechisms* (Nashville: B&H, 1996). A fine survey of the historical record of the church is found in Dever, "The Church," in *A Theology for the Church*, ed. Daniel L. Akin, (Nashville: Broadman and Holman Academics, 2007), 816–37.
16. Greg Wills, "The Church: Baptist and Their Churches in the 18th and 19th Centuries," in *Polity: A Collection of Historic Baptist Documents*, ed. Mark E. Dever (Washington, DC: Center for Church Reform, 2001), 21.
17. W. L. Lumpkin, *Baptist Confessions of Faith* (Valley Forge: Judson, 1959; rev. ed. 1969), 365–66.
18. Mark Dever, *Nine Marks of a Healthy Church* (Wheaton: Crossway, 2000), 212.

CHAPTER 2

1. "First Council of Constantinople (A.D. 381): Creed," *New Advent* [cited 11 February 2008]. Available from the Internet: *www.newadvent.org/fathers/3808/htm*.
2. Mark Dever, "The Church," in *A Theology for the Church*, ed. Daniel L. Akin, (Nashville: Broadman and Holman Academic, 2007), 776. This section on the historical perspective is indebted to Dever's excellent treatment (775–78).
3. Ibid.
4. John Calvin, *Analysis of the Institutes of the Christian Religion*, ed. and trans. Ford Lewis Battles, LCC (Philadelphia: Westimister, 1960), 4.1.17, 286.
5. Dever, "The Church," 777.
6. Ibid.
7. Ibid., 778.
8. Ibid.
9. Martin Luther, "On the Councils and the Church," in *Martin Luther's Basic Theological Writings*, ed. Timothy Lull (Minneapolis: Fortress, 1989), 547.
10. John Hammett, *Biblical Foundations for Baptist Churches* (Grand Rapids: Kregel, 2005), 63.
11. John Calvin, *Analysis*, 4.1.9: 1023.
12. Hammett, *Biblical Foundations*, 63.
13. J. D. Freeman, "The Place of Baptists in the Christian Church," *The Baptist World Congress: London, July 11–19, 1905, Authorized Record of Proceedings* (London: Baptist Union Publication Department, 1905, 27, as quoted in Hammett, *Biblical Foundations*, 82. Hammett's superb chapter (4) on "Regenerate Church Membership" (81–108) is very helpful.
14. Hammett, *Biblical Foundations*, 84.
15. Stan Norman, "Ecclesiological Guidelines to Inform Southern Baptist Church Planters," position paper presented to the North

American Mission Board, September 28, 2004, 15–16.

16. See Robert Stein, "Baptist and Becoming a Christian in the New Testament," *Southern Baptist Journal of Theology*, vol. 2., no. 1 (Spring 1998): 6–17.

17. Ibid., 14. Stein highlights the significance of the latter aspect.

18. "Baptism and the Lord's Supper," *The Baptist Faith and Message* (Nashville: LifeWay Press, 2000), 14.

19. Text and commentary can be found in Daniel L. Akin, "An Expositional Analysis of the Schleitheim Confession," *Criswell Theological Review* 2.2 (1988): 356.

20. Stephen Prothero, "A Nation of Faith and Religious Illiterates," *Los Angeles Times* [online], 12 January 2005 [cited 7 February 2008]. Available from the Internet: *www.latimes.com*.

21. *Baptist Faith and Message*, 13.

22. See Chad Brand and R. Stanton Norman, eds., *The Perspectives on Church Government: Five Views on Church Polity* (Nashville: Broadman & Holman, 2004).

23. One need only survey W. L. Lumpkin, *Baptist Confession of Faith* (Valley Forge: Judson, 1959, rev. ed. 1969). Also see Daniel Akin, "The Single-Elder-Led Church" in Brand and Norman, 57–59.

24. Chris Turner, "Draper Expounds on Young Ministers' Involvement, Decline in Baptisms," *Facts & Trends* (Nashville: LifeWay Press, Jan.–Feb. 2005), 26–29.

25. His address, "Three Changes in Theological Institutions," is summarized and analyzed in John A. Broadus, *A Gentleman and a Scholar: A Memoir of James Petigru Boyce* (Birmingham: Solid Ground Christian Books, 1893), 120–45.

26. Ibid., 122. Also see 132.

27. Ibid., 139.

CHAPTER 3

1. For a summary of these positions, see Millard Erickson, *Christian Theology*, 2nd ed. (Grand Rapids: Baker, 1998, 1080-94; Wayne Grudem, *Systematic Theology* (Grand Rapids: Zondervan, 1994), 923–36; Leon Morris, "Church Government," *Evangelical Dictionary of Theology*, 2nd ed. (Grand Rapids: Baker, 2001), 256–58.

2. D. A. Carson, Matthew, *Expositor's Bible Commentary*, vol. 8 (Grand Rapids: Zondervan, 1984), 402–3.

3. Ibid.

4. Mark Dever, *Nine Marks of a Healthy Church* (Wheaton: Crossways, 2000), 221.

5. There is a textual issue related to this phrase. Some translations, such as the NASB, read, "The apostles and the brethren who are elders" or something similar. We have followed the HCSB, believing it better reflects the overall context at this point.

6. Gordon D. Fee, *New International Commentary on the New Testament: The First Epistle to the Corinthians* (Grand Rapids: Eerdmans, 1987), 206. Fee goes on to state, "In this text church discipline is not the affair of one or a few. Even though Paul as an apostle pronounced the sentence prophetically, the sin itself was known by all and had contaminated the whole; so the action was to be the affair of all" (213–14).

7. Colin Kruse, *Tyndale New Testament Commentary: 2 Corinthians*, (Grand Rapids: Eerdmans, 1987), 81–82.

8. Reformers such as Luther affirmed two marks of the church: (1) the Word rightly preached and (2) the sacraments (ordinances) rightly administered.

9. Robert Saucy, *The Church in God's Program* (Chicago: Moody, 1927), 116.

10. Dever, *Nine Marks*, 222.

11. D. A. Carson, "Authority in the Church," in *Evangelical Dictionary of Theology*, 2nd ed. (Grand Rapids: Baker, 2001), 249.

12. Timothy George, "The Priesthood of All Believers and the Quest for Theological Integrity," *Criswell Theological Review* 3.2 (1989): 285. This section on the priesthood of believers is indebted to this article and draws significantly from it.

13. Ibid., 286–87.

14. Ibid., 291.

15. Those who hold this view include J. B. Lightfoot, *St. Paul's Epistle to the Philippians* (London: MacMillian, 1981), 95–99; Herman Ridderbos, *Paul: An Outline of His Theology*, trans. John R. de Witt (Grand Rapids: Eerdmans, 1975), 457; D. A. Carson, Douglas J. Moo, and Leon Morris, *An Introduction to the New Testament* (Grand Rapids: Zondervan, 1992), 364; E. Earle Ellis, *Pauline Theology: Ministry and Society* (Grand Rapids: Eerdmans, 1989), 103; George Knight, *The Pastoral Epistles, New International Greek Testament Commentary* (Grand Rapids: Eerdmans; Carlisle, England: Paternoster, 1992), 175–77; William D. Mounce, *Pastoral Epistles, Word Biblical Commentary*, vol. 46 (Nashville: Nelson, 2000), 161–63.

16. Jerome Letter 69.3, trans. W. H. Fremantle with the assistance of G. Lewis and W. G. Martley under the title *The Principle Works of St. Jerome, Nicene and Post-Nicene Fathers*, vol. 6, 2nd series (Grand Rapids: Eerdmans, 1952), 143. Lightfoot adds, "But, though more full than other writers, [Jerome] is hardly more explicit. Of his predecessors the Ambrosian Hilary had discerned the same truth. Of his contemporaries and successors, Chrysostom, Pelagius, Theodore of Mopsuestia, Theodoret, all acknowledge it. Thus in every one of the extant commentaries on the epistles containing the crucial passages, whether Greek or Latin, before the close of the fifth century, this identity is affirmed" (Philippians, 99).

17. B. Spencer Haygood, "Pastor," Trent Butler, ed., *Holman Illustrated Bible Dictionary* (Nashville: Holman Bible, 2003), 1250.

18. Consult Benjamin L. Merkle, "The Elder and Overseer: One Office in the Early Church." (Ph.D. dissertation, The Southern Baptist Theological Seminary, 2000). Much of our discussion in this section is significantly dependent on and guided by Merkle.

19. See John H. Armstrong, *The Stain That Stays* (Scotland: Christian Focus, 2000); Warren W. Wiersbe, *The Integrity Crisis* (Nashville: Nelson, 1988, 1991).

20. How the church in Jerusalem could have done this is impossible to imagine, given that it began with three thousand converts on Pentecost (see Acts 2:40-27). Although many of these converts lived outside Jerusalem (see Acts 2:9-11), a large number must have resided in the city.

21. Mark Dever, *A Display of God's Glory* (Washington, DC: Center for Church Reform, 2001), 23.

22. Methodists like Asbury and Cartwright actually pioneered this method of caring for churches on the American frontier. See "Circuit Rider," "Francis Asbury," and "Peter Cartwright," in J. D. Douglas, ed., *The New International Dictionary of the Christian Church* (Grand Rapids: Zondervan, 1978); R. G. Tuttle, "Circuit Rider," in Daniel G. Reid, ed., *Dictionary of Christianity in America* (Downers Grove: InterVarsity Press, 1990), 280–81.

23. Gordon D. Fee, "Reflections on Church Order in the Pastoral Epistles, with Futher Reflection on the Hermeneutics of Ad Hoc Documents," *Journal of Evangelical Theological Society*, 28 (1985): 149.

24. Daniel L. Akin, *1, 2, 3 John, New American Commentary* (Nashville: Broadman & Holman, 2001), 245–49.

25. Dever, *Nine Marks*, 218.

26. James T. Draper Jr., *We Believe* (Nashville: LifeWay Press, 2003), 58–59.

27. Carson, "Authority in the Church," 250.

28. Thom Rainer, *Effective Evangelistic Churches* (Nashville: Broadman & Holman, 1996); *High Expectations* (Nashville: Broadman & Holman, 1999); *Surprising Insights from the Unchurched* (Grand Rapids: Zondervan, 2001).

29. Edmund P. Clowney, *The Church* (Downers Grove, IL: Intervarsity Press, 1995), 202.

CHAPTER 4

1. J. L. Dagg, *Manual of Theology, Second Part: A Treatise on Church Order* (Charleston: The Southern Baptist Publication Society, 1858), 274.

2. Mark Dever, "The Church," in *A Theology for the Church*, ed. Daniel L. Akin (Nashville: Broadman and Holman Academics, 2007), 806.

3. R. Albert Mohler, "Church Discipline: The Missing Mark," *Southern Baptist Journal of Theology*, 4.4 (Winter 2000): footnote 2, 26–27.

4 Text and commentary can be found in Daniel L. Akin, "An Expositional Analysis of the Schleitheim Confession," *Criswell Theological Review*, 2.2 (1988): 356–57.

5. Greg Wills, "Southern Baptist and Church Discipline," *Southern Baptist Journal of Theology*, 4.4 (Winter 2000): 9–10.

6. Ibid., 10.

7. Ibid.

8. Dietrich Bonhoeffer, *Life Together* (New York: Harper and Row, 1954), 107.

9 Frank E. Gaebelein, ed., *Ephesians-Philemon, Expositor's Bible Commentary*, vol. 11 (Grand Rapids: Zondervan, 1978), 447.

10. D. Edmond Hiebert, *Titus and Philemon* (Chicago Moody, 1957), 75.

11. John MacArthur, *The MacArthur New Testament Commentary: Titus* (Chicago: Moody, 1996), 164.

12. Dever, "The Church," 808.

13. Bonhoeffer, *Life Together*, 107.

14. Thomas D. Lea and Haynes P. Griffin Jr., *1, 2 Timothy and Titus*, New American Commentary (Nashville: Broadman and Holman, 1992), 331.

15. MacArthur, *Titus*, 167.

16. Tony Evans, *God's Glorius Church: The Mystery and Mission of the Body of Christ* (Chicago: Moody, 2003), 222.

17. Charles Finney, *Lectures to Professing Christians* (New York & London: Garland Publishing, Inc., 1985), 45.

18. Mark Dever, *Nine Marks of a Healthy Church*, expanded ed. (Wheaton: Crossway, 2004), 166.

19. R. Kent Hughes and Bryan Chapell, *1 & 2 Timothy and Titus: To Guard the Deposit* (Wheaton: Crossway, 2000), 364.

20. Thomas C. Oden, *Corrective Love: The Power of Common Discipline* (St. Louis: Concordia, 1995), 47.

CHAPTER 5

1 Mark Dever, "The Church," in *A Theology for the Church*, ed. Daniel L. Akin (Nashville: Broadman and Holman Academics, 2007), 809.

2. Curtis Vaughn, *Acts* (Grand Rapids: Zondervan, 1974), 25.

3. John Polhill, *Acts* (Nashville: Broadman & Holman, 1992), footnotes 111–12.

4. Sidney Greidanus, *The Modern Preacher and the Ancient Text: Interpreting and Preaching Biblical Literature* (Grand Rapids: Eerdmans, 1988), 12.

5 John Albert Bengel, *Gnomon of the New Testament*, ed. Andrew R. Fausset, 5 vols. (Edinburg: Clark, 1857–58), 1:7, cited by Walt Kaiser, *Toward an Exegetical Theology* (Grand Rapids: Baker, 1981), 7.

6. John Stott, *Acts* (Downers Grove: InterVarsity Press, 1990), 82.

7. *Barna Report*, Spring 1998.

8. Thom S. Rainer, "A Resurgence Not Yet Realized: Evangelistic Effectiveness in the Southern Baptist Convention since 1979," *The Southern Baptist Journal of Theology* (2005), 62.

9. Polhill, *Acts*, 122.

10. Warren Wiersbe, *Be Dynamic* (Wheaton: Victor, 1988), 34.

CHAPTER 6

1. Millard J. Erikson, Church Theology, 2nd ed. (Grand Rapids: Baker, 1998), 1038.

2. Kent Hughes, *Ephesians* (Wheaton: Crossway, 1990), 121.

3 John MacArthur, *Ephesians* (Chicago: Moody, 1986), 119.

4. Warren Wiersbe, *Be Rich* (Wheaton: Victor, 1981), 96–97.

5 Ibid., 97.

6. Curtis Vaughn, *Founders Study Guide Commentary: Ephesians* (Cape Coral: Founders, 2002), 89.

LEADER PREPARATION

This guide will help you prepare to lead a six-session, small-group study of this book. Step-by-step plans for leading each session are suggested in the leader guide that follows each chapter:

LEARNING GOALS

This study will help participants—

- gain a better understanding of biblical teachings on the church;
- identify the blessings and benefits of church membership;
- gain a deeper appreciation and love for the church;
- strengthen their commitment to the church.

ADVANCE PLANNING

1. Schedule the study for a time that allows as many people as possible to attend. A minimum of six one-hour sessions are needed to complete the study. The study could be scheduled for a series of Sunday evenings or Wednesday evenings, or it could be conducted on a series of weekdays or weeknights. You may need to plan activities for other age groups who are not involved in this study.

2. Promote the study through your church newsletter and bulletin, announcements in worship services and Adult Sunday School classes, and electronic communication.

3. Order a copy of this book (item 005125346) for each participant. Distribute the books in advance and ask members to read chapter 1 and complete the learning activities before the first group session.

4. There is no substitute for intensive study and preparation. Read the book several times, highlighting key statements. Teaching ideas may come to you as you read. Jot these down in the margins. Complete all of the learning activities. Examine the leader guides that follow the chapters.

5. Make prayer a vital part of your preparation. Pray that God will help you as you lead the group. Pray for the persons who will attend the study.

6. Gather the resources you will need. You will need a supply of three-by-five-inch cards, large sheets of paper or poster board, masking tape, and felt-tip markers.

7. If you would like to display a course poster throughout the study, make one by list-
ing the chapter titles from the contents page (p. 3) on poster board.

PREPARING FOR EACH SESSION

1. Study in detail the chapter for the session, along with the leader guide that follows
the chapter. You will probably find more teaching suggestions than you will have
time to use during the session. Select the activities that will best meet the needs of
your group. Decide whether you need to adapt any activities.
2. Prepare any group assignments you will need for the session.
3. Arrange the meeting room before the session begins. The room arrangement should
create an atmosphere conducive to learning. For example, seating participants in a
semicircle rather than in rows will encourage interaction.
4. Pray for each group session and for each participant.

LEADING EACH SESSION

1. Arrive early to greet members as they arrive. Start and stop on time. Begin and close
each session with prayer.
2. During the session try to create a relaxed atmosphere that helps everyone feel a
sense of belonging. Show a caring, loving spirit. Be sensitive to the needs of the
group. Be willing to adapt and change your teaching plans as necessary.
3. Involve participants in the study. Do not talk too much and do not be afraid of peri-
ods of silence. Do not rush the activities. Be flexible, but do not allow the discussion
to wander. Keep the focus on the subject at hand. Encourage members to share their
insights, experiences, questions, and feelings.
4. Suggestions in this guide call for dividing into small groups from time to time. The
ideal group size is three or four persons. If there are not enough members for the
number of groups suggested, combine some of the assignments. If there are more
than enough members for the number of groups suggested, divide into more groups
and give duplicate assignments.
5. Magnify the Bible during the sessions. Encourage participants to memorize Scripture during the study. Verses for memorization are suggested at the beginning of
each chapter.
6. Encourage participants to read the chapters and to complete the learning activities
in order to gain the most from the study.

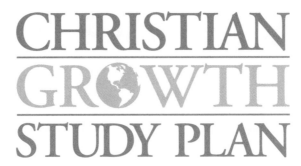

CHRISTIAN GROWTH STUDY PLAN

In the Christian Growth Study Plan, *Vibrant Church* is the resource for course CG-1376 in the subject areas The Church and Ministry in the Christian Growth category of diploma plans.

To receive credit, read the book, complete the learning activities; attend group sessions, show your work to your pastor, aq staff member, or a church leader; then complete this form. This page may be duplicated. Send the completed form to:

Christian Growth Study Plan;
One LifeWay Plaza; Nashville, TN 37234-0117;
Fax (615) 251-5067; e-mail *cgspnet@lifeway.com*.

For information about the Christian Growth Study Plan, refer to the current *Christian Growth Study Plan Catalog*, located online at *www.lifeway.com/cgsp*. If you do not have access to the Internet, contact the Christian Growth Study Plan office, (800) 968-5519, for the specific plan you need for your ministry.

VIBRANT CHURCH
Course CG-1376
PARTICIPANT INFORMATION

Social Security Number (USA ONLY-optional)	Personal CGSP Number*	Date of Birth (MONTH, DAY, YEAR)

Name (First, Middle, Last)	Home Phone

Address (Street, Route, or P.O. Box)	City, State, or Province	Zip/Postal Code

Email Address for CGSP use

Please check appropriate box: ❑ Resource purchased by church   ❑ Resource purchased by self   ❑ Other

CHURCH INFORMATION

Church Name

Address (Street, Route, or P.O. Box)	City, State, or Province	Zip/Postal Code

CHANGE REQUEST ONLY

☐ Former Name

☐ Former Address	City, State, or Province	Zip/Postal Code

☐ Former Church	City, State, or Province	Zip/Postal Code

Signature of Pastor, Conference Leader, or Other Church Leader	Date

*New participants are requested but not required to give SS# and date of birth. Existing participants, please give CGSP# when using SS# for the first time. Thereafter, only one ID# is required. **Mail to:** Christian Growth Study Plan, One LifeWay Plaza, Nashville, TN 37234-0117. Fax: (615)251-5067.

Revised 4-05